THE SAS POCKET MANUAL 1941–1945

Compiled and Introduced by
Christopher Westhorp

BLOOMSBURY
LONDON • NEW DELHI • NEW YORK • SYDNEY

Conway
An imprint of Bloomsbury Publishing Plc

50 Bedford Square
London
WC1B 3DP
UK

1385 Broadway
New York
NY 10018
USA

www.bloomsbury.com

CONWAY™ is a trademark and imprint of Bloomsbury Publishing Plc

First published 2015

British Library Cataloguing-in-Publication Data
A catalogue record for this book is available from the British Library.

Library of Congress Cataloguing-in-Publication data has been applied for.

ISBN: HB: 978-1-8448-6259-7
ePDF: 978-1-8448-6293-1
ePub: 978-1-8448-6294-8

FSC www.fsc.org
MIX
Paper from responsible sources
FSC® C020471

2 4 6 8 10 9 7 5 3 1

Designed by CE Marketing
Printed and bound in Great Britain by CPI Group (UK) Ltd, Croydon CR0 4YY

To find out more about our authors and books visit www.bloomsbury.com. Here you will find extracts, author interviews, details of forthcoming events and the option to sign up for our newsletters.

CONTENTS

INTRODUCTION

'Who Dares Wins' is arguably the most famous motto in the British Army, forming part of the insignia of what is now one of the best-known military formations in the world. At the same time as the words imply courage and derring-do, they also neatly sum up the foundation story of the regiment: a heretical proposal led to the creation of a small-force warfare unit that brilliantly anticipated the asymmetrical warfare of the post-war era.

The 'Special Air Service' (SAS) thus arose against the odds from unorthodox channels and it was never entirely accepted by those who shared a more conventional military mind-set. Few records exist from the SAS's earliest days, but this book is not a detailed regimental history; neither is it a full operational survey of the SAS's exceptional war record. What follows are documents of historical interest – internal memorandums, on-the-record reminiscences, training documents and contemporary manuals and journalism – that have been selected because they represent essential elements of the SAS story, revealing fascinating things about important aspects of training and key pieces of equipment, as well as the experiences of personnel when putting theories into practice at the sharp end. Together, this material gives some insights into why these soldiers were to earn the name 'special forces'.

ROOTS OF A RADICAL IDEA

Before the Second World War, experience of the so-called colonial 'small wars' had led many military theorists to write about the effectiveness of partisan forms of warfare. Within the War Office in Whitehall, Military Intelligence (Research) or MI(R), under the leadership of Lieutenant Colonel J.F.C. Holland, was interested by the potential military value of

an irregular warfare capacity as an adjunct to conventional capabilities. Lieutenant Colonel Colin McVean Gubbins was given responsibility for developing tactics and training outside orthodox British Army doctrines. Like Holland, he had experience of security operations against IRA guerrillas in Ireland, as well as a spell in Russia in 1919 working with the White Army anti-Bolshevik forces during the Russian Civil War. Gubbins duly devised a radical new set of teachings, which he distilled into three training pamphlets in collaboration with explosives expert Millis Jefferis: 'The Art of Guerrilla Warfare', 'The Partisan Leader's Handbook' and 'How to Use High Explosives'. In 1940 Gubbins raised the Independent Companies and formed the Auxiliary Units, in anticipation of the need for a resistance movement in the wake of an expected German invasion.

'The Art of Guerilla Warfare' set out the general principles of such a creed, placing a value on fresh ideas, ceaseless activity and the importance of using resources effectively, as well as strategies – 'executed with audacity' – for making enemy-held territory ungovernable, which included sabotage as a potent part of the war effort. Such ideas were then realised through specialist units created to wage war within enemy-occupied territory. The patterns of many SAS activities in France in 1944, including linking up with local forces, were quite clearly foreshadowed in Gubbins's pamphlet. He identified 83 principles, but in Chapter 1 only four sections, with 11 principles, have been selected as relevant here (Objectives of Guerilla Warfare, Methods and Principles, Arms and Equipment, Geographical) with several excerpts from the Conclusion.

The idea of taking the initiative through proactive warfare was an inspiration for those Allied servicemen who yearned to strike at the enemy after the Fall of France. Gubbins argued that small, well-led units using speed, stealth and surprise could be effective against superior forces, and by 1940 these strands of thought had given rise to the Commando concept. These ideas underpinned the courses at the Special Training Centre (STC) established at Lochailort and elsewhere in the

western Scottish Highlands – courses and centres that expanded as the war progressed.

The STC was manned by a group of military and civilian specialists who imparted their knowledge and expertise to all those who passed through: from marksmanship and weapons-handling skills to unarmed combat and demolitions. Making good use of the old boys' network, one of the earliest members of the training staff was an acquaintance of Gubbins: Captain William ('Bill') Stirling, who was later to become head of 2nd SAS. Stirling's younger brother, David, also trained and was briefly a fieldcraft instructor at Lochailort. The Stirling brothers, Mike Calvert (who, in 1940, produced his own pamphlet 'The Operations of Small Forces Behind the Enemy Lines') and others were typical of a new generation of creative military thinkers and doers, many of whom had emerged initially as Commandos before contributing to the further development of the philosophy and small-force ethos that would produce the SAS.

THE STRATEGIC VISION

A former Scots Guards' officer, Lieutenant David Stirling had served with No.8 (Guards) Commando and then the ad hoc Special Service Brigade known as Layforce (Commando), where he learned to operate behind enemy lines. However, after several operational setbacks and with a deteriorating strategic position in the Mediterranean in 1941, it was decided to disband Layforce. Stirling, though, was convinced that the basic concept of Layforce remained a good one and he felt there was a strategic requirement for a different kind of versatile military formation – a new, deep-penetration raiding force.

Within the vastness of the North Africa theatre, Stirling was quick to appreciate just how much havoc a group of adventurous, resourceful and highly manoeuvrable men could cause if it was on the loose within the enemy's rear, at liberty to inflict a disproportionate amount of damage and immobilise thousands of enemy troops in the process. Whereas the Commandos were used (and sometimes misused) principally in tactical roles, and reliant on naval support that was not being adequately exploited, Stirling argued for a concept that was strategic and flexible. He proposed saboteur groups of just five (later four) men, to be inserted by air, land (using the Long Range Desert Group, or LRDG) or sea, who would inflict damage on enemy airfields equivalent to a Commando force 40 times larger. Or, to think of it in another way, instead of 200 men attacking one objective, 40 to 50 groups of determined men, using guile and surprise, could carry out that many destructive attacks simultaneously. The task of such a new unit was, he believed, to influence the course of the war as a whole rather than tactically affecting particular battles. Stirling's magical formula was intended to use minimum manpower to produce 'maximum possibilities of surprise'.

Stirling appreciated that, in addition to delivery by land and sea, a practicable method of aerial insertion was a key part of his proposition. Encouraged by Brigadier Laycock, he began testing parachuting methods with his friend Jock Lewes. After one such drop Stirling found himself laid up in a Cairo hospital bed. This period of recuperation was the key moment in the development of the SAS concept, because out of it emerged a radical memorandum – now existing only as he recalled it later – that Stirling delivered to the Middle East Headquarters (MEHQ). Ever the maverick, he did so personally, without appointment, deliberately bypassing the official channels that he believed would snuff out the idea at gestation.

Stirling sketched a vision of a specially organised, specially equipped and specially trained unit, which could act covertly and be infiltrated (by land, sea or air) to operate behind enemy lines. Stressing the bedrock organisational principle of the (by then) four-man sub-unit (a pair of couples – a dynamic that he felt was important in the forging of intense kinship bonds), and the avoidance of leadership in the top-down

traditional sense, he later explained that from its outset the SAS had had some firmly held tenets from which it should never depart:

1. The unrelenting pursuit of excellence.

2. The maintaining of the highest standards of discipline in all aspects of the daily life of the S.A.S. soldier, from the occasional precision drilling on the parade ground even to his personal turnout on leave. We always reckoned that a high standard of self-discipline in each soldier was the only effective foundation for Regimental discipline. Commitment to the S.A.S. pursuit of excellence becomes a sham if any *single one* of the disciplinary standards is allowed to slip.

3. The S.A.S. brooks no sense of class and, particularly, not among the wives. This might sound a bit portentous but it epitomizes the S.A.S. philosophy. The traditional idea of a crack regiment was one officered by the aristocracy and, indeed, these regiments deservedly won great renown for their dependability and their gallantry in wartime and for their parade-ground panache in peacetime. In the S.A.S. we share with the Brigade of Guards a deep respect for quality, but we have an entirely different outlook. We believe, as did the ancient Greeks who originated the word 'aristocracy', that every man with the right attitude and talents, regardless of birth and riches, has a capacity in his own lifetime of reaching that status in its truest sense; in fact, in our S.A.S. context, an individual soldier might prefer to go on serving as an NCO rather than have to leave the Regiment in order to obtain an officer's commission. All ranks in the S.A.S. are of 'one company' in which a sense of class is both alien and ludicrous. A visit to the Sergeant's Mess at S.A.S.

HQ in Hereford vividly conveys what I mean.

4. Humility and humour: both these virtues are indispensable in the everyday lives of officers and men – particularly so in the case of the S.A.S. which is often regarded as an élite Regiment. Without frequent recourse to humour and humility, our special status could cause resentment in other units of the British Army and an unbecoming conceit and big-headedness in our own soldiers.[1]

The modest proposal seemed to combine the individual élan of the cavalry with the collective spirit of the everyman age. Auchinleck, Commander-in-Chief Middle East, endorsed it and the new unit first emerged in July 1941 as 'L' Detachment, Special Air Service (SAS) Brigade. After the war Stirling produced a memorandum, 'History of the SAS', that was used at the staff college in Camberley. His summary of operations is featured here (in Chapter 3), prefaced with pieces on the proposal, the origin of the name, recruitment and training (points 7–21 inclusive, of the original 22-point memorandum). It is unclear whether Stirling's proposal emerged from within a more general debate about the need to motivate and inspire Allied soldiers, but a 1942 memorandum from within the Middle East Commando suggests that there were some discussions along those lines. The memo-writer, Lieutenant Colonel Laycock, identified that the modern army was in need of the infusion of a new spirit. He argued that the British admired 'honour, courage, and self-discipline' and yearned for the infusion of a 'spirit of adventure', the solution to which was 'inspiration through action' – something that, thanks to Stirling, the SAS was already demonstrating:

In a previous paper on minor raiding a policy of action was suggested by which men of the regular army could get to grips

with the enemy. The percentage initially effected would be small, but the results would soon be enormous. If fifty men only saw action each week the spirit would spread like wildfire. If the men employed were leaders, or future leaders, it would spread even faster, because of the many new sources of contact made possible by the genius of the age.

There remains now one other question only – what sort, what type, of action? Why should such action differ in any way from other actions of the war? Such action differs in spirit, and in the way it is approached. These raids, almost of a pirate nature, are small and very personal. There is in them an element of cheek, another English characteristic. They are performed by skill – not by force – skill, daring, and initiative. They rely on no outside help, no complicated modern machinery. They are, in very essence, more of a crusade than a nerve-shattering modern battle, where men, the servants of great machines, feel they are no more than cogs. Such action appeals to the individual man, to his muscles, his spirit, his imagination. He, and he alone, must face the enemy with a great and over-riding self assurance. He is taught to improvise, to use his wits, to rely on himself only. He is taught that the impossible is not always impossible but sometimes the most practical of all.

This is not mere theorising. It is the result of practical experience. The spirit exists in this unit. On the lines of the previous paper on raiding it must be allowed to spread. Our Army lacks the spirit of adventure, the key to a deeper spirit, for that spark, once lit, leads on and on to a faith outside itself. Nazi Germany has fashioned a creed which men will live and die for, for which it is considered a privilege to die to defend or advance that creed. Bestial though it is it serves its purpose, it welds the army as one. Hitler, through his own evil genius,

> has appealed to the genius of Germany. Against that white-hot fanaticism we match a feeble flame, while deep down in [our] nature ... there is ample fuel to feed it. Drake made good his wildest boasts for he appealed to the genius of the nation, cheek, adventure, the love of the sea, the scorn of hardship and danger. That spirit made us what we were before it ebbed and faltered. That spirit must be raised again if we are to keep our place.[2]

'THESE MEN ARE DANGEROUS'

Promoted to captain, and reporting directly to Auchinleck, Stirling recruited many men from the remains of Layforce, albeit not without difficulty because elements in MEHQ treated the new formation like a renegade pariah. Of his officers, Stirling always acknowledged the original role of 'Jock' Lewes, formerly of the Welsh Guards, and Blair 'Paddy' Mayne, formerly of the Irish Guards, as co-founders of the regiment. In 1985, giving a speech at the opening of the Stirling Lines (SAS headquarters), Stirling referred to having always felt uneasy for being known as the founder of the regiment, which he felt had five co-founders. As well as Lewes and Mayne, he named Georges Bergé (sometimes spelled Berget), founder of the French SAS, and (post-war) Brian Franks and John Woodhouse.[3]

In autumn 1941, the earliest SAS recruits – encouraged by a Stirling wager and, characteristically, ignoring the official channels – competed before their first operation to create a distinctive beret, badge and motto that would foster unity and pride in their new formation. It was also hoped that having such things would curb any tendency to act rough and tough, which some critics (including Stirling, however unfairly) had levelled at the early Commandos. Aggression was to be reserved for the enemy. According to one of the 'originals', Reg Seekings, an early suggestion was 'We Descend To Defend'.[4] The badge with the

parachutist's wings, designed by 'Jock' Lewes, was inspired by winged scarabs in Egypt – specifically decorations within the Shepheard's Hotel in Cairo. The beret insignia is a flaming Excalibur, designed by Bob Tait, but his 'Strike & Destroy' motto was replaced by Stirling's own aristocratically inspired 'Who Dares Wins', which Randolph Churchill claimed he would better but never did. The badge is the one still worn today.

On 17 November 1941 'L' Detachment's first parachute operation was described by Stirling as 'a complete failure'. However, after that inauspicious debut, which exposed the shortcomings of airborne operations, a fuller collaboration with the LRDG was born and from then on vehicles, especially Jeeps, were used as the means to and from the deep-penetration target area. Eventually the SAS acquired desert navigation skills and its own specially modified Jeep transportation, which enabled the remaining SAS, just a few dozen strong, to embark upon a series of destructive raids in 1941–1942 against enemy airfields and important logistical points throughout North Africa.

These raids were characterised by bravado, flair and inventiveness. Although the attrition rates, due to capture or death, could be significant, for those missions that succeeded there was no denying the data of destruction: approximately 400 Axis planes in North Africa were put out of action, which was more than the RAF managed. SAS Major Blair 'Paddy' Mayne accomplished more aircraft 'kills' than any fighter pilot in the desert war. Some of the most entertaining insights come from the reminiscences of those who survived to tell the less glorious tales: such as the escapades during a Benghazi raid recalled in a letter by Randolph Churchill, son of the Prime Minister (reproduced in Chapter 4).

The daring exploits of Britain's new battlefield warriors were even celebrated as 'super-commandos' in the July 1942 edition of *The American Magazine*, which published an article by its roving war correspondent Gordon Gaskill. Hitler was quick to note the effect the SAS had been having and issued an instruction to German forces: '... these men are very dangerous, and the presence of S.A.S troops in any area must be immediately reported ... they must be ruthlessly exterminated.'

As a result of its spectacular and disproportionate achievements the SAS was re-expanded, given a squadron of Free French paratroopers,[5] whom Stirling later described as 'the bravest of the brave', and new equipment. While in the ascendant, in August 1942 Stirling proposed to Churchill that all the Special Service units in the Middle East should come under his command, including Layforce's surviving Folbot Troop. All this was approved and by October 1942 'L' Detachment had been officially designated 1st SAS Regiment, with squadrons that included a Special Boat section under the command of George Earl Jellicoe, the French already mentioned, and the Greek Sacred Squadron. By December 1942 the SAS had more than 500 officers and other ranks, and by 1944 it would total approximately 2,500 all ranks.

EXPANSION AND REORGANISATION

David Stirling's brother, Lieutenant Colonel 'Bill' Stirling, of 62 Commando, had persuaded the command in Algiers that he should raise a second SAS regiment to support the First Army in North Africa, which was duly formed as 2nd SAS Regiment in January 1943. Unfortunately, that same month David's battlefield luck ran out when he was captured in Tunisia (naturally, he didn't conform and in due course had to be consigned to Colditz). The remnants of the 1st SAS Regiment then had its Special Boat sections reorganised as the Special Boat Squadron (rechristened Special Boat Service in November and moved to Raiding Forces Middle East, but retaining the SAS insignia, to conduct amphibious sabotage), still under Jellicoe, who argued there was potential in small-scale raiding in the Mediterranean Basin (see Chapter 6). A Special Raiding Squadron (SRS) was created under Major Mayne.

From a small unit of Jeep-mobile raiders in the desert the SAS had begun

to assume a more complicated and diverse role, though the philosophy and operational principles remained steadfast. Both the Special Raiding Squadron and the 2nd SAS Regiment played a significant strategic role in the Allied campaign in the Mediterranean, spearheading the Allied landings in Sicily and the Italian mainland, working collaboratively with the partisans and operating to great effect – ambushing Axis convoys of reinforcements and destroying railway links – far ahead of the Allied front line as it was pushed north. Meanwhile, acting within the operational structure of the SBS, SAS members harassed German forces throughout the Aegean and Adriatic. Mayne received the first of three Bars to his DSO during Operation HUSKY because of, as the citation put it, his 'courage, determination and superb leadership' during the actions near Syracuse and at Augusta in July 1943.

Until January 1943 the French sections had undertaken raiding missions alongside the LRDG and SAS. One notable seaborne raid was mounted in mid-June 1942 by a group of five, plus a Greek guide, against Heraklion, Crete, to try to hamper air attacks against the Malta convoys. The five, led by Bergé himself, included four Frenchmen and the French-speaking Jellicoe. After planting their charges on 21 aircraft, which they watched detonate later that night, they made their way to the beach. While Jellicoe was away to signal for the submarine pick-up, the French party was discovered or betrayed and, despite putting up fierce resistance, all four were captured or killed.

Early in 1944 both SAS regiments returned to the UK and were constituted in March as the 1st SAS Brigade, under Brigadier Roderick McLeod, as part of Airborne Corps. The brigade also included two Free French SAS Battalions (3rd and 4th), a Belgian Independent Parachute Company (5th SAS), the Greek Sacred Squadron and a unit known as GHQ Reconnaissance Regiment (Phantom), or signalling section, for communications. Although the SAS had established its battlefield reputation in North Africa, it was to be the French connection, so to speak, where the regiment's strategic contribution was arguably the most far reaching. Both in terms of the manpower component and the crucial theatre of operations, France in 1944 proved to be a vindication of the SAS idea and the scene of both regimental triumph and tragedy.

TRAINING

The first in-theatre training camp for the SAS was established at Kabrit, in the Egyptian desert. As touched upon earlier, many of the earliest SAS men were former Commandos, mainly Layforce, who at that stage of the war (before 1942) had received their special training in the western Highlands, which would have been at the Special Training Centre (STC) at Lochailort. Instructors had to pass all of the Lochailort course before they could teach it. The chief instructor there, until late 1940, was William ('Bill') Stirling; and in June 1940, as mentioned earlier, his younger brother David had served briefly there.[6] As well as the Stirlings, other later senior SAS men also trained or instructed there, including Fitzroy Maclean and Mike Calvert, who at one time was the STC's demolitions instructor. Although Stirling stressed that the SAS was different from the Commandos, any initial differences lay in principles and organisation rather than the practical skills needed for small-force guerilla warfare. Stirling wanted disciplined toughness, powers of endurance, and training 'designed to foster discipline, skill, intelligence, courage, fitness, determination'.

Anxious themselves for action in the war, many of the earliest instructors had left the STC in order to practise the special operations they had been teaching. Desert survival and navigation skills may have been specifically tailored to the Western Desert theatre, as well as parachute instruction, but it seems reasonable to conclude that the STC's irregular warfare training syllabus provided an influential model for at least some of the earliest special operations training conducted elsewhere, just as it did for courses run in Australia and Singapore.

Originated to cause havoc as saboteurs behind enemy lines, SAS soldiers needed to be experts in the art of offensive demolitions. The skilled exploitation of explosives was a core part of the training programme developed for the special training centres in Scotland and given the vital importance of this art to the SAS, in laying waste to enemy transportation and supply lines, the training course notes from Lochailort, dated March 1941, are interesting to read. Both Lecture 1 'Explosives & How to Fire Them' and Lecture 6 on 'General Destruction', from the five-day course on 'Offensive Demolitions', are informative.

'Jock' Lewes was in charge of the training at Kabrit and his lasting contribution to explosives was the invention of a compact, light, field incendiary device known as the 'Sticky' or 'Lewes' bomb. Having found other devices unreliable, he had experimented until he arrived at a mix containing a quarter-pound of thermite, a pound of Nobel No. 808 plasticine-like explosive and an amount of flammable liquid (motor oil) with a small amount of gun cotton primer and a detonator. Placed in a cloth container and stuck to a plane near the fuel tanks, the new bomb (used with a delayed-action fuse) was a potent weapon during airfield raids.

In Scotland, practical exercises included the placing of concealed pressure switch charges on the railway to derail a train and trips to industrial installations to learn most effectively how to put them out of action. For Calvert, who was to command the SAS towards the end of the war in Europe, the experience at Lochailort was a compelling insight into 'the means of destroying a vital strategic point which for some reason or other the main force could not reach ... [the small force] could dart in quickly ... and do their deadly work before the other side really knew what was going on.'[7] Apart from the destruction of the objective itself, a further strategic purpose of demolitions – as Gubbins had specified – was to encourage the enemy to spread his forces around in an attempt to guard potential targets against attack, thus tying them down on security duties.

Derrick Harrison, who had fought at Salerno with 1st SAS (or SRS), recalled his own experience of training in Scotland as a brigade alongside the French and Belgian SAS men, before embarking on operations in France with 1st SAS. For three months they had undergone stamina, night-time and sabotage training, learning from power station officials and railwaymen 'how we could cause the most damage with the least trouble to ourselves, from large-scale demolitions to nuisance-value sabotage'.[8] He noted that: 'There were many little difficulties to overcome, of course. There were no textbooks on S.A.S. work. Everything had been developed in the light of experience and from our mistakes. The whole fund of knowledge of this type of work lay in the minds of the 'old operatives'.'[9]

Tellingly, Harrison made a more general observation about the overall effectiveness and distinctiveness of SAS training:

> Everything possible was done to encourage individuality and initiative. Officers and men received the same training so that, in the event of only one man of a party surviving, he should be equipped to go ahead and finish the job himself. A new relationship was fostered between officers and men, based on mutual respect and real friendship. That, with the ability to live with one's fellows, was indispensable when small groups of men were required to live, sometimes for months at a stretch, in the heart of enemy territory. Never before were the opposites of individuality and team work so successfully wedded together.[10]

WELL ARMED AND HIGHLY MOBILE

SAS members were trained to use all manner of Allied weapons and were also familiar with Axis firearms. Reliability and firepower were two key requirements. Rather than any of the British rifles, the American carbines had admirers because they were lighter and reasonably accurate, especially the M1 and M1A1 (folding-stock version) carbines. The British

Sten submachine gun was light but was considered unreliable, whereas the American Thompson was felt to be sturdy and dependable. The Bren light machine gun had many admirers. Based on a modified Czech design, originally produced in Brno, the Bren was a gas-operated light machine gun that was portable and reliable; although it could overheat when firing its 500 rounds per minute of .303-inch ammunition, it had a quick-change barrel. It weighed about 25 pounds (with a magazine) and was usually fired when prone (as demonstrated in the British Army's training pamplet), but it could be used with a sling and fired quite readily from the hip when advancing. The Bren had a distinctive curved box magazine; it was fitted with a bipod but it could also be vehicle-mounted or fitted with a tripod. (See Chapter 8 The Bren Light Machine Gun: Description Use and Mechanism.)

'Small Arms Training Pamphlet No. 4 Light Machine Gun', from 1942, demonstrates for instructors how to make use of cover when laying down fire with an LMG, figures 10–16.

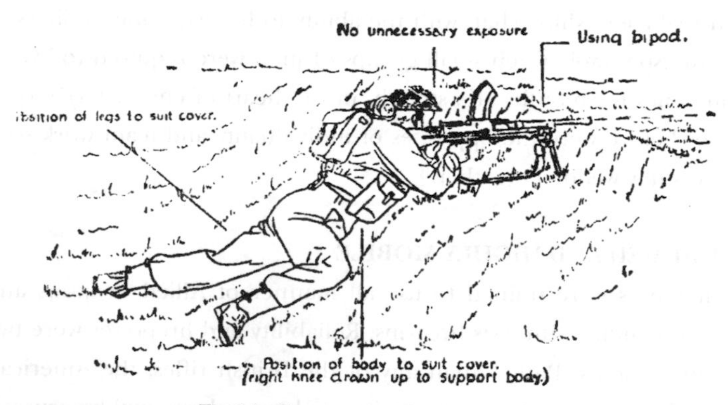

Fig 10. Gun mounted using Bipod.

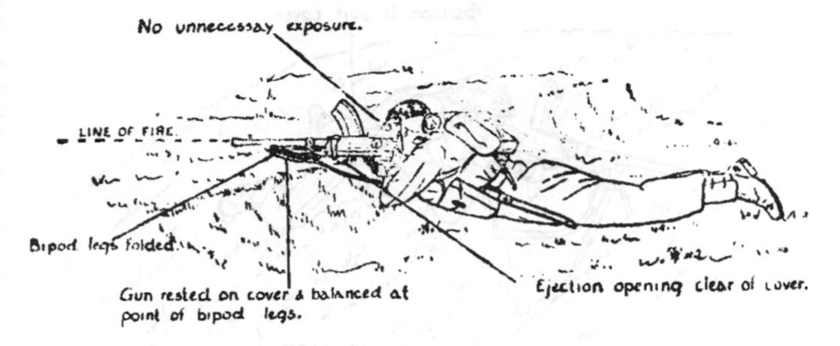

Fig 11. Gun mounted without use of Bipod.

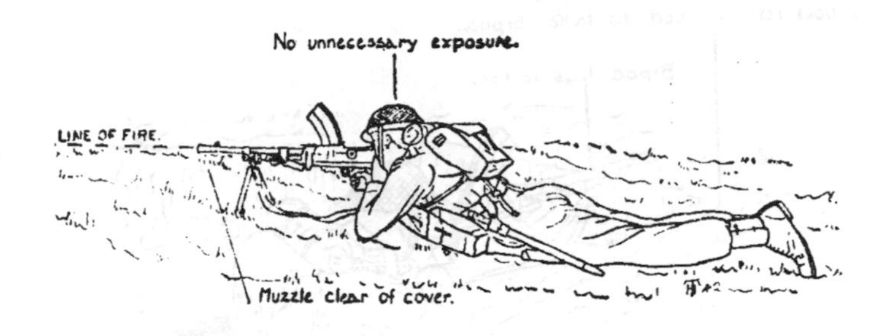

Fig 12. Gun mounted using a fold in the ground.

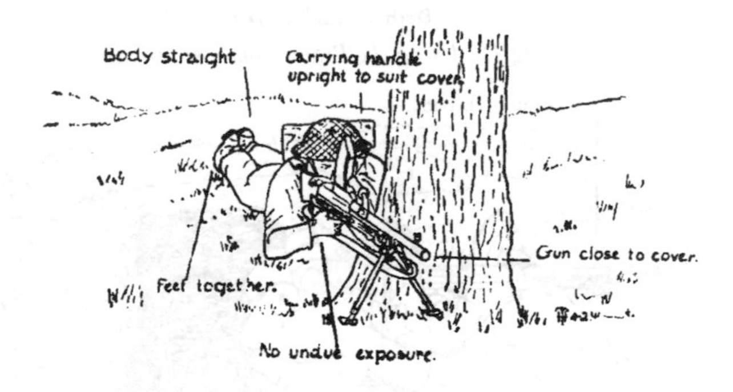

Fig 13. Gun mounted round isolated cover.

Fig 14. Gun mounted on the side of a slope.

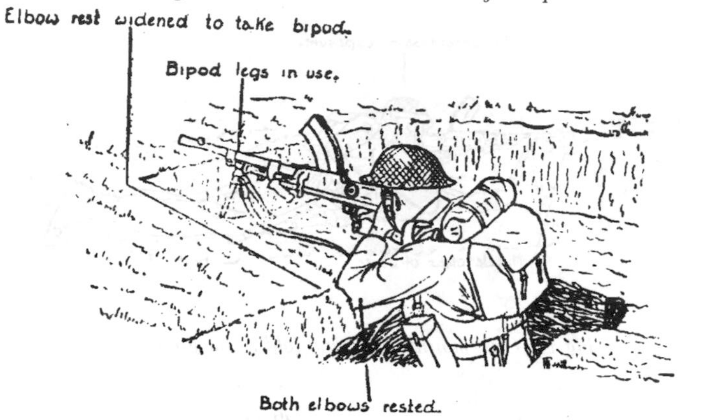

Fig 15. Using the Bipod from a slit trench.

Fig 16. Without the use of the Bipod from a slit trench.

However, possibly the most iconic of all machine guns used by the SAS was one adopted from Britain's Royal Air Force (RAF): the Vickers Class K machine gun, also known as the VGO (Vickers Gas Operated). It was developed out of the French Berthier light machine gun, which was similar to the Bren. Vickers thought that the Class K could replace the Lewis gun, but when the British Army instead adopted the Bren, the Vickers Berthier gun was adapted into the Vickers K to create a weapon suitable for flexible mountings in aircraft.

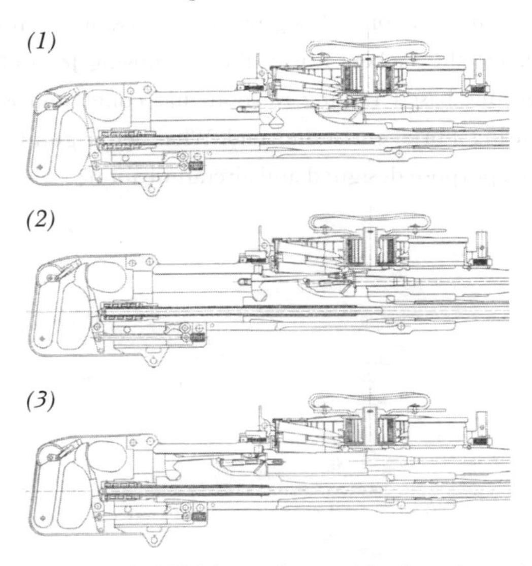

FLIGHT *magazine in July 1939 featured an article about the compactness and high rate of fire of the Vickers K machine gun, which it lauded as a modern aircraft gun. The K gun's unique features and action were explained using a three-part diagram. In (1) the piston and breech block have been propelled forwards by the force of the compressed main spring. The cartridge has been fired by the piston having pushed the firing pin forwards. In (2) the piston and breech block have started to move back, propelled by gases deflected from the muzzle, which then re-compresses the spring. In (3) the piston and breech block are rearmost, with the piston at rest against the buffer and about to go forwards. During the rearwards movement of the breech block the empty case is extracted and ejected into a bag on the side of the gun.*

Complete with flash eliminator, the gun was 40 inches long, and, fitted with sights, deflector and bag, weighed 22 pounds. Although normally used by the aircraft observer as a directly operated free gun, the Model K could have remote control for turret or wing mounting, or could be fitted with a stock for ground-defence purposes. The LRDG mounted it on the dashboard of their Jeeps as a main armament and the SAS followed suit. As the turret-mounted Browning began to replace the Vickers as RAF aircraft armament, the 303-inch calibre Class Ks became readily available for use as ground weapons. Being practical, mission-oriented soldiers, the SAS married the Vickers K with the fast-moving Jeep platform and created a ground-based raiding weapon that could unleash awesome firepower during a brief-encounter raid. What better gun to use against aircraft than a purpose-designed anti-aircraft weapon?

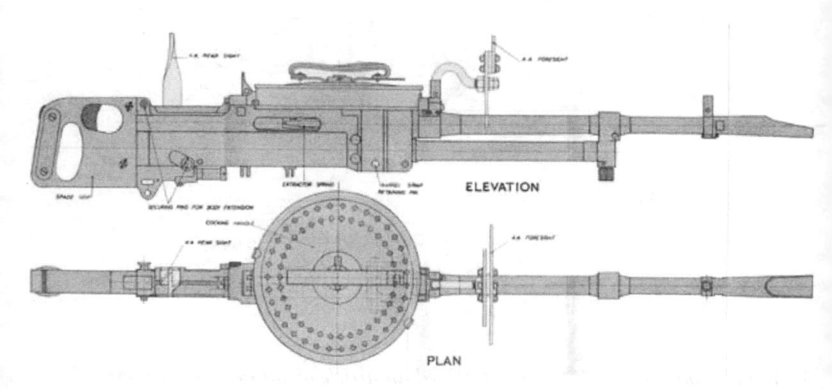

This general arrangement diagram of the Vickers, showing a side elevation and plan, is from B.R. 776 Handbook for Vickers .303-inch G.O. No. I Mark I Gun on the Mark III, IV and V Mountings, *dated 1943.*

The Vickers K was described shortly before the war (27 July 1939) in *FLIGHT* magazine as 'probably the most successful gun of its type in the world'. The article explained how the 'exceptionally compact' weapon had a muzzle velocity of 2,400 feet per second and a high rate of fire of between 950 and 1,200 rounds a minute. The unusually smooth action, combined with a low recoil force, made the gun easy to control and aim with accuracy. There were no external moving parts, which might injure the gunner, and the gun had a minimum of exposed surface. Ammunition was fed from a spring-loaded drum magazine, which normally held 60 or 100 rounds, but for fixed installation it could accommodate 300 or 600 rounds in very large, flat magazines. The gun could be dismantled in a few seconds with the aid of a cartridge and a penknife.

The design of the breech block enabled the gun's rate of fire to be adjusted to more than 1,000 rounds per minute. A handicap for the infantry, because of the ammunition consumption, but an advantage when vehicle-mounted and used against other softskinned vehicles or stationary aircraft. *Flight* featured several diagrams to demonstrate the action of the Vickers K.

Bob Bennett recalled the Vickers K as '… formidable. … Terrific guns. You loaded them with one round of armour-piercing, a round of tracer, armour piercing, ball. A fantastic gun.'[11] Johnny Cooper claimed to have been the first SAS man to fire the Vickers K, during the successful raid against oil tanker lorries and storage facilities at the German-held port of Bouerat in January 1942. When they were ambushed on the way out he simply 'let rip'. He recalled: 'Stirling was on the back of the truck and he said to me afterwards: 'Young Cooper, that's a marvellous weapon."[12]

The ultra-mobile and sturdy vehicle that the SAS found perfect for its purpose was the Willys Jeep MB. The US Army had a requirement for a light, four-wheel drive general-purpose vehicle and scout car. In July 1940 it had sent out its specification to more than 130 American firms, giving them 11 days to bid. The specification was highly demanding: contained within a rectangular body, with a folding windshield, three seats and blackout lighting, it had to have four-wheel drive with a front-driving axle and a two-speed transfer unit. Its engine had to be capable of 85 pound-foot (115 Newton metres) of torque with a speed of 50 mph, while its

weight (originally) was restricted to 1,300 pounds and it had to be able to carry a 660-pound load including a .30-inch calibre machine gun.

Initially, only a few companies were able to respond. The Willys-Overland entry offered 105 pounds of torque compared to its Bantam and Ford competitors', 83 and 85 pounds, respectively. The weight requirement was relaxed (2,160 pounds) and all three companies were contracted to deliver models by June 1941. The final production model was a hybrid design, produced and engined by Willys with its rugged and reliable 'Go Devil' engine of 60 horsepower. Hundreds of thousands of Jeep MBs were built from 1941 to 1945, with General George C. Marshall calling it 'America's greatest contribution to modern warfare'. (See Chapter 7 Willy's Manual 1944.)

Jeeps proved far superior to parachutes and the means par excellence for carrying out the deep-penetration raids envisaged by Sterling as his unit's raison d'etre. Indeed, one of the most iconic images of the wartime regiment is a Jeep in the desert – armed with Vickers gas-operated machine guns – driven by wild-looking, bearded SAS men. The Vickers K machine guns were usually mounted in pairs and, including the Browning, up to five guns were found on many vehicles, enabling a single Jeep to unleash thousands of rounds in a few minutes. Possession of the heavily armed Jeep meant that it was no longer as essential to place delayed explosives charges – a lightning-fast, shoot-em-up raid targeting the parked aircraft could be carried out if required.

This technique was discovered in the field as an improvisation. The first SAS raids using Jeeps took place in early July 1942, during the withdrawal to the El Alamein line while they were initially still working alongside LRDG. During a simultaneous attack on multiple airfields in the Fuka, El Daba and Bagush areas, only half the charges placed by Mayne on 40 aircraft had actually detonated. Stirling's immediate solution to the problem was the rapid drive-by shooting. The thrill and daring of it had a galvanising effect on all the SAS men. The story also reveals an essential aspect of the SAS, repeated a myriad times in France in 1944: real warfare rarely goes according to plan – success and survival often depend on the use of initiative.

By July 1942 the SAS had become fully motorised and equipped with both Jeep MBs and four-wheeled trucks. The LRDG had trained the SAS in all the arts of driving in the desert and, as Stirling's memorandum confirms, the 'astonishing agility of the jeep enabled us to approach a target at night over almost any country'. The Jeeps were specially modified in theatre, not only to cope with the machine gun mounts, but also to: remove any parts deemed non-essential for the mission; strengthen the springs; add extra armour; fit a water condenser to the radiator; customise storage for the carrying of extra water, fuel and ammunition supplies; and so on.

With their own Jeeps the SAS were able to mount month-long missions behind the lines and even before Stirling's capture, his small, highly motivated group of men had embarked on a serious wrecking spree. By November 1942, around 400 aircraft had been destroyed.

THE FRONT MOVES TO NORTHWEST EUROPE

As the crucial western fronts had moved from Africa then to Italy and on into northwestern Europe, the SAS more often led than followed. Under Roderick McLeod, Brian Franks, Mike Calvert and others, the SAS played a key part behind the enemy lines before, during and after the Normandy landings in June 1944. Rather than the short-term – and sometimes costly – raids beloved by the conventional planners, the SAS Brigade commander fought hard to ensure it retained its strategic role and remained at the forefront of the action. This was achieved by parachuting into occupied France and assisting the French Resistance with supplies and training, as well as working alongside Allied Jedburgh units and in collaboration with the local Resistance groups to mount diversionary attacks and other missions to further the strategic aims of

the Supreme Headquarters Allied Expeditionary Forces (SHAEF).

From Brittany in the east to the Vosges in the west (where many captured SAS men were brutally executed), Ardennes in the north and Rhône (near Lyon) further south, the SAS established dozens of support missions and operational bases, from which it carried out a widespread campaign of sabotage to hinder the enemy's capacity to wage war effectively – especially targeted was the transportation network: railway lines and bridges were blown, roads mined and convoys ambushed. SAS units would also pinpoint targets for RAF bombing raids.

Generally, a small reconnaissance party would be inserted and if all the conditions were supportive, reinforcements and supplies were sent, which might include armoured Jeeps. In central France (between Orleans and Dijon) in particular, four operational bases were established from which Jeep-patrols could range and ravage the German units and essential infrastructure in the area. The four were code-named KIPLING (1st SAS, 14 August–25 September), WALLACE (2nd SAS, 19 August–19 September), NEWTON (1st SAS and 3rd SAS, 19 August–11 September) and SPENSER (4th SAS, 29 August–14 September). As happened elsewhere, these bases and activities were sometimes extended to complement any other wide-ranging and successful ongoing operations, such as HOUNDSWORTH, which was active near Dijon from immediately after D-Day. A report appears here (as Chapter 11) of casualties inflicted by the SAS.

Greatly to his credit, Brigadier McLeod established a complex network of communications operated by the Phantom signals squadron that enabled the huge scale of operations to be overseen and coordinated from Brigade HQ in London. Naturally, given the technology of the time and the fluid nature of things in the combat zones, these communications were prone to interruption and the effect of this is revealed in the report from Major Cary-Elwes (reproduced as Chapter 9), who went into Brittany in June 1944 after contact had been lost with some of the elements which had established the bases named SAMWEST and DINGSON, as detailed in the report of operations by 4th SAS, which is also reproduced here (Chapter 10).

Dropped into France as a vital part of the D-Day invasion plan, 4th (French) SAS was tasked with cutting off and destroying German resistance in central Brittany, harassing enemy communications and with identifying and arming French Resistance groups. The so-called Cooney teams within 4th SAS were to cut the railway lines in order to impede the German response to both D-Day and the offensives that would follow in its wake. Bases in the Morbihan and Cotes du Nord areas (code-named DINGSON and SAMWEST respectively) were established from which the SAS and Maquisards inflicted many casualties, but the experience proved costly and the SAS thereafter avoided concentrations, dispersed into small groups and kept on the move.

By August the SAS had received thousands of supply drops and armed and organised more than 6,000 men into nine battalions. By early August the Germans had concentrated into three pockets of resistance in Brittany. When 3rd SAS attacked one of those, in Brest, it took 5,000 prisoners before linking with US 4th Armored Division. Advancing north to cut off the German retreat, by mid-September when operations south of the Loire ended 4th SAS had taken more than 12,000 prisoners. In December 1944 4th SAS was transferred to Ardennes, where they assisted the Americans until the end of January 1945.

The SAS then served with great distinction in Belgium, the Netherlands (which included the airborne drop AMHERST) and Germany until the end of the war in Europe. In Schleswig-Holstein, only weeks before the war ended, Mayne earned the third bar to his DSO. Meanwhile, having returned from Colditz, Stirling became deputy commander of the SAS Brigade in July 1945. The next month, the 1st and 2nd SAS regiments returned from a short-lived operation (DOOMSDAY) to disarm German troops in Norway, before, in October 1945, the SAS Brigade

was disbanded, in spite of a detailed memorandum about the unit's effectiveness (extracts of which form Chapter 12).

THE LEGEND LIVES ON

There is a temptation to assess the effectiveness of the SAS by roll-calling the statistics of wartime destruction, such as the numbers of aircraft destroyed, enemy killed or captured, trains and bridges destroyed, and so on. And that data of damage was, of course, important. However, as intuited by both Stirling and Laycock, in another respect the greatest impact that the creation and actions of the regiment had was psychological: the enemy was unsettled, destabilised and disoriented by the whirlwind of phantoms in its midst, while the Allies were given real confidence and a positive reinforcing belief that if they could match the SAS for persistence, professionalism and pluck, they would carry the day – who dared, won.

NOTES

1. From Stirling's memorandum reminiscences as cited in these sources: Geraghty, Tony. *Who Dares Wins: The Special Air Service, 1950 to the Falklands.* Arms and Armour Press: London, 1980, page 9. Strawson, John. *A History of the S.A.S. Regiment.* Secker & Warburg: London, 1984, pages 247–248.
2. Selected extracts from a memorandum entitled 'Discipline and morale. The need for a new spirit' by Lieutenant Colonel Laycock, commander of Special Service Brigade Layforce and Middle East Commando, 24 August 1942. From the papers of Major General Sir Robert Edward Laycock (1907–1968), 'Draft publications, scripts and press cuttings relating to Laycock and Special Service Brigade', reference LAYCOCK 8/16, LHCMA.
3. From Stevens, Gordon. *The Originals: The Secret History of the Birth of the SAS.* Ebury Press: London, 2006, pages 335–338.
4. From *The Originals*, 2006, page 56.
5. By September 1940 the Free French in England had formed, under Lieutenant Georges Bergé, 1ère Compagnie d'Infanterie de l'Air des Forces Francaises Libre (1ère CIA), which began infiltration missions into occupied France in 1941. In January 1942 the Free French were formed into a squadron and attached to 'L' Detachment SAS Brigade in Egypt, commanded by Major David Stirling. Ultimately they were incorporated by 1944 in the SAS Brigade as 3rd SAS, sometimes referred to as 3rd French Para Bn. A second Free French unit became 4th SAS, or 4th French Para Bn.
6. Many of the recruits to both the Commandos and SAS attended those courses, which were inspired by a select group of men – a complex, interconnected nexus of 5th Scots Guards, MI(R), pre-war gentlemen skiers and mountaineers – some of whom, such as William ('Bill') Stirling, became SAS commanders. (The fieldcraft exercises related to evasion techniques seem to have owed something to Highland stalking techniques.)
7. Cited in Allan, page 51: Calvert, M. *Fighting Mad: One Man's Guerrilla War.* Jarrolds: London, 1964, page 49.
8. From Harrison, D.I. *These Men are Dangerous: The S.A.S. at War.* Cassell & Co.: London, 1957, p.113.
9. From *These Men are Dangerous*, 1957, page 108.
10. From *These Men are Dangerous*, 1957, introduction p.xiii.
11. From *The Originals*, 2006, page 132.
12. From *The Originals*, 2006, page 100.

CHAPTER 1

THE ART OF GUERILLA WARFARE GENERAL PRINCIPLES

C.M. Gubbins, 1939

Selected points 8–16, 34, 74 and 79–81

Objectives of Guerilla Warfare

8. The whole art of guerilla warfare lies in striking the enemy where he least expects it, and yet where he is most vulnerable: this will produce the greatest effect in inducing, and even compelling, him to use up large numbers of troops guarding against such blows.

Modern large-sized armies, entirely dependent as they are on the regular delivery of supplies, munitions, petrol. etc., for their operations, present a particularly favourable opportunity for guerilla warfare, directed against their communications by road, rail or water, and against their system of internal postal and telegraph communications.

Further, the maintenance of these large armies necessitates the establishment of dumps and stocks of supplies, munitions, etc. at focal points, which offer most suitable targets for guerilla action.

The guarding of these communications and dumps against attack will, even before the threat is evident, necessitate the institution by the enemy of detachments and posts, more particularly at vital points on the communications and where dumps of importance are located. These detachments themselves are a suitable object of attack.

Thus the operations of guerillas will usually be directed against the flanks of armies, against their communications and against posts and detachments established by the enemy for the express purpose of protecting his important localities against such sporadic attempts.

Methods and Principles

9. The methods and principles of guerilla warfare must be based on a proper estimation of the relative advantages and disadvantages enjoyed by the enemy on one hand, and the guerillas on the other, in armaments,

mobility, numbers, information, morale, training, etc.

10. The enemy will almost invariably possess armaments superior both in quantity and quality—i.e., he will have artillery, mortars, gas, armoured vehicles, etc., in addition to the automatics and rifles with which the guerillas will also be armed. In total strength the enemy will normally have the superiority as well, but the distribution of his forces will necessitate the use of detachments against which superior guerilla forces can be brought.

11. It is in mobility, in information, and in morale that the guerillas can secure the advantage, and those factors are the means by which the enemy's superior armament and numbers can best be combatted. The superior mobility, however, is not absolute, but relative—i.e. to the type of country in which the activities are staged, to the detailed knowledge of that country by the guerillas, etc. In absolute mobility, the enemy must always have the advantage—i.e., the use of railway systems, the possession of large numbers of motors, lorries, armoured cars, tanks, etc., of large forces of cavalry, etc. By the judicious selection of ground, however, and by moves in darkness to secure surprise, the guerillas can enjoy relatively superior mobility for the period necessary for each operation.

12. The enemy will usually be in a country where the population is largely hostile, so that the people will actively co-operate in providing information for the guerillas and withholding it from the enemy. The proper encouragement of this natural situation and the development of the system of obtaining information will ensure that the guerillas are kept au fait with the enemy's movements and intentions, whereas their own are hidden from him.

13. Morale, training, etc., are factors of importance in which first one side and then the other may have the advantage. Where the enemy is constrained by demands on his forces to use reserve and second-line units for guarding communications etc., neither the morale nor training will be of a high standard. The morale of the guerilla should always be high; fighting in his own country, among his own people, against a foreign foe who has invaded his land, the justice of his cause will inflame his embitterment. At the same time, the narrow limits of the training he requires, his natural dash and courage, and the careful, detailed rehearsal of projected coups should enable him, with the advantage of the initiative, to match even the best trained troops.

14. Guerillas must obtain and make every effort to retain the initiative. To have the initiative confers the invaluable advantage of selecting the place

of operations that most favour success as regards locality, ground, time, relative strengths, etc. The initiative can always be secured by remaining completely quiescent until the moment for the commencement of guerilla activities arrives, and then suddenly launching out against an unsuspecting enemy. To retain the initiative conferring these advantages demands a ceaseless activity, so that the enemy is prevented from getting in his blow by the constantly recurring necessity of parrying those aimed at him.

15. Until the final and culminating stages of partisan warfare where large bodies of guerilla are co-operating with the regular forces, it must be the object of partisans to avoid prolonged engagements with their opponents, unless in such overwhelming strength that success can be assured before the arrival of reinforcements. The object must be to strike hard and disappear before the enemy can recover and strike back. Therefore, the action of all partisan bands must be governed by the necessity of a secure line of retirement for use when the moment for calling off the action arrives. It must be borne in mind, too, that the immunity of partisans from enemy action is a most valuable moral factor; to inflict damage and death on the enemy and to escape scot-free has an irritant and depressing effect on the enemy's spirit, and a correspondingly encouraging effect on the morale, not only of the guerillas but of the local inhabitants, a matter of considerable moment; in this sphere of action nothing succeeds like success.

16. From the above review of the circumstances of guerilla warfare, the aim of the guerillas must be to develop their inherent advantages so as to nullify those of the enemy. The principles of this type of warfare are therefore: –

(a) Surprise first and foremost, by finding out the enemy's plans and concealing your own intentions and movements.

(b) Never undertake an operation unless certain of success owing to careful planning and good information. Break off the action when it becomes too risky to continue.

(c) Ensure that a secure line of retreat is always available.

(d) Choose areas and localities for action where your mobility will be superior to that of the enemy, owing to better knowledge of the country, lighter equipment, etc.

(e) Confine all movements as much as possible to the hours of darkness.

(f) Never engage in a pitched battle unless in overwhelming strength and thus sure of success.

(g) Avoid being pinned down in a battle by the enemy's superior forces or armament; break off the action before such a situation can develop.
(h) Retain the initiative at all costs by redoubling activities when the enemy commences counter-measures.
(i) When the time for action comes, act with the greatest boldness and audacity. The partisan's motto is "Valiant yet vigilant."

These are the nine points of the guerilla's creed.

Arms and Equipment

34. The arms most suitable for guerillas are those which do not hamper their mobility, but which are effective at close quarters. Guerilla actions will usually take place at point blank range as the result of an ambush or raid, with the object of inflicting the maximum amount of damage in a short time and then getting away. What is important therefore is a heavy volume of fire developed immediately, with the object of causing as many casualties and consequent confusion as possible at the outset of the action. Undoubtedly, therefore, the most effective weapon for the guerilla is the sub-machine gun which can be fired either from a rest or from the shoulder—i.e. a tommy-gun or gangster gun; in addition, this gun has the qualities of being short and comparatively light. Special efforts must therefore be made to equip each band with a percentage of these guns. Carbines are suitable, being shorter and lighter than rifles, and the long range of the rifle is not necessary. After carbines come revolvers and pistols for night work and for very close quarters, and then rifles. The more silencers that can be obtained for these weapons the better; a 'silenced' rifle or revolver not only impedes detection, but has a considerable moral effect on the sniping of sentries, etc. Telescopic sights are invaluable for snipers.

Bayonets are quite unsuitable for guerillas; these are only for use in shock action which should be eschewed; a dagger is much more effective, and more easily concealed.

Bombs and devices of various kinds are of great use; when possible they should be specially made for the peculiar requirements of guerilla warfare, but standard army equipment must frequently be made to serve.

Geographical

74. The geographical study of a territory is concerned with two factors:
(a) Its suitability as an area for guerilla warfare. The more broken and forested it is, the more suitable will it be.

(b) The potential targets for guerilla action which it offers. These will usually be in the shape of road, rail and river communications which the enemy would have to employ for the maintenance of his armies in the field. Vulnerable points within the enemy's own territory must also be marked. The reconnaissance of territories should whenever possible be carried out in time of peace by selected officers who have been grounded in the principles of guerilla warfare. Their reports will be of great assistance in formulating a plan.

Conclusion

79. These operations range over an unlimited field according to local circumstances. Large forces of guerillas can harry the flanks of an advancing or returning army, can raid his communications in force, destroying railways, burning supply dumps and capturing convoys, and then withdraw again to the security of their own lines. Small bands of partisans can live behind the enemy's lines, or filter through gaps in his front, and carry on similar activities on a smaller scale. Individual guerillas can be permanently located in the enemy's rear, where by the sniping of guards, the destruction of military vehicles, buildings, etc., they can be a running sore in his flesh, draining his vitality and hampering his action.

80. Guerillas obtain their advantage over the enemy by their greater knowledge of the country, their relatively greater mobility, and their vastly superior sources of information. Those are the factors which, when properly exploited, enable them to engage with success an enemy who is better equipped, more closely disciplined, and usually in greater strength.

81. The main objects of guerilla warfare are to inflict direct damage and loss on the enemy, to hamper his operations and movements by attacks on his communications, and to compel him to withdraw the maximum number of troops from the main front of battle so as to weaken his offensive power. Direct action of the types envisaged will bring the desired result about. It must always be remembered that guerilla warfare is what regular armies have most to fear. When directed with skill and carried out with courage and whole-hearted endeavour, an effective campaign by the enemy becomes almost impossible.

CHAPTER 2

OFFENSIVE DEMOLITIONS
LOCHAILORT FIELDCRAFT COURSE

Lectures 1 and 6
(December 1940, January 1941, March 1941)

THE COURSE

Lecture 1.	Explosives & How to Fire Them	1 hour
Practical 1.	Firing Explosives	2 ½ hours
Lecture 2.	The Main Charge	1 hour
Practical 2.	Firing Large Charges	3½ hours
Lecture 3.	Mechanisms, Bombs & Incendiary	1 hour
Practical 3.	Mechanisms, Bombs & Incendiary	3½ hours
Lecture 4.	The Scope of Explosives	1 hour
Practical 4.	Placing Charges	2½ hours
Lecture 5.	Raids	1 hour
	The Wrecker	1½ hours
	Demonstration Raid	1½ hours
Lecture 6.	General Destruction	1 hour
	Examination & Discussion	2 hours
		22 hours

Lecture 1
EXPLOSIVES & HOW TO FIRE THEM

1. INTRODUCTION.

THE OBJECT OF THIS COURSE IS TO TEACH YOU TO DESTROY THINGS QUICKLY.

It is unnecessary to emphasise the necessity of this knowledge to irregular troops. Take a raid for instance. Its object is not often to obtain information, for we have agents to do that. Certainly not to kill the enemy, for that would be a mere drop in the ocean. Not usually to capture prisoners, they are seldom worth the trouble. Surely if the raid is to be of real military value its object will nearly always be the destruction of anything important to the enemy's war effort – communications, transport, ships, docks, planes, weapons, ammunition, food. Only by destruction of this nature can small parties of men deal the enemy a really effective blow.

In the past, destruction has been left almost entirely to the R.E., and certainly a knowledge of construction is a good start. But now, you cannot rely on having the R.E. with you – there are more opportunities for the use of this powerful weapon than there are R.E. to go round, – so you must assume the responsibility yourselves.

It is not asking too much. Destruction is an ordinary human instinct, and we teach you here far more than any Sapper was ever taught about quick destruction. And at the end of the Course, we believe that you will be competent to take on, and confident of taking on, any ordinary quick destructive job. The only case where you must always give way to a Sapper is where the objective is large and complicated, and his technical engineering knowledge will come in, (e.g. – reinforced concrete structure).

Destruction can be achieved with explosives, fire, or by various methods of sabotage; and by using certain mechanisms and booby traps the principle of war of surprise can be introduced. We go into all that; but for security reasons we call the whole course "Demolitions".

Like everything else here, you must learn it with the object of passing it on to your men; and to help you teach them we give out, at the end of the course, precis of our lectures and a demonstration box of stores to each unit represented.

We begin now with the more orthodox side of demolitions – how to destroy things quite simply with explosives.

2. WHAT IS AN EXPLOSIVE ?

An explosive is a substance (usually a solid) which is chemically unstable and is trying to turn itself into a gas. The chemist makes it in this state, and he can turn it out as unstable as he likes. But if the explosive is very unstable it may suddenly become a gas at an inconvenient moment, so obviously for practical purposes they make it reasonably stable or safe.

3. DETONATION.

In order to change suddenly into gas, an explosive requires some extra "fillip" from outside, and this fillip must be great heat, great shock, or a little of both. The process of change is called detonation.

Detonation is a complete and sudden change, like the Pumpkins in Cinderella. It is quite different from burning, which is a comparatively slow change. There are some explosives which burn, like Gunpowder and Cordite, and they are called Low Explosives; but in demolition work we deal only with High Explosives which detonate.

Modern high explosives are made so stable that they can be handled quite safely. They can be dropped, kicked, hit hard with wood and generally treated roughly, and even a naked flame is unlikely to cause detonation; but sparks, hot cinders, glowing cigarette ash or friction against metal are dangerous. If detonation is caused the explosion will not spread across an air gap, so that separate cases of explosives will not all go off together unless they are in very close contact, or in a confined space.

4. THE DETONATOR.

In order to detonate the explosive when required a detonator is used. This is a small quantity of very sensitive or unstable explosive – so sensitive that it can easily be set off when required by the heat from a burning fuse or glowing wire. The detonator is about as sensitive as a wrist watch – it can be dropped on grass but not on concrete, it can be handled firmly but not bent or hit, and you must on no account interfere with the works inside. But there is so little explosive in it, that going off alone a detonator would only blow off a finger or two.

5. THE PRIMER.

In fact there is so little explosive in the detonator that it does not even produce enough shock to detonate most common explosives, so the shock has to be stepped up with a primer. A primer is a small quantity of

explosive (one oz) which is certain to be detonated by the detonator, i.e. – it is less stable than the main explosive. The primer is put somewhere in the middle of the main explosive and the detonator is put in the middle of the primer.

If the main explosive or main charge, which may be of 100 lbs. or more, is all in contact, only one primer and detonator are required, to let the whole lot off.

6. SAFETY FUSE.

The detonator may be initiated either by fuse or electrically. An electric detonator has two wires sticking out of it and it is detonated by passing a current through it (either way) from a battery, accumulator, mains or an exploder. An ordinary detonator has an open end into which a length of safety fuse ("Bickford") is inserted. The other end of the safety fuse is lit with a match.

Safety fuse is really a train of gunpowder, only it is enclosed inside a waterproof tube instead of being laid along the floor out of a barrel as in the best films. It is made to burn at 2 ft. a minute, so remembering that you walk normally 100 yards in one minute, you can use just as much as you require to get away to a place of safety.

7. HIGH EXPLOSIVES.

Now to get back to the explosives themselves, and in order to be able to deal with any which may be met, it is convenient to divide all explosives for recognition purposes into Slabs, Powders and Cartridges. All ordinary explosives are made in one of these forms, although at first sight they may be disguised in metal containers etc.

SLABS.

Made in 1 lb. slabs or bricks, with a tapered hole in the center to take the primer. All slab explosives are very stable, and even a rifle bullet will not detonate them. They will work if they get wet, but not if they are wet through – i.e. they will only survive say one hour's immersion. The usual ones are Gun Cotton (white) and T. N. T. (yellow).

POWDERS.

Of the consistency of sand. Like the slabs, they are very safe and are not detonated by a rifle bullet. They become quite useless if at all damp, so they are often packed in little waterproof bags. The most common is Ammonal (light or dark grey). Picric Acid or Melinite (yellow) is another powder explosive, and T. N. T. (yellow) is also sometimes made in this form.

CARTRIDGES.

These include nearly all the common commercial explosives. They are all soft or rubbery or putty-like, and are made in 4 oz. cartridges wrapped in waxed paper or cellophane. They are not damaged by damp. They are, generally speaking, less safe or stable than the Slabs or Powders, and are likely to be detonated by rifle bullets. In the same way, many of them may be detonated by the detonator alone with no primer, but this is not advised.

This last group includes all the nitro-glycerine explosives – Dynamite (reddish-brown, fudge-like, out of date), Blasting Gelatine (yellow jelly), Gelignite (buff, granular, putty-like) and 808 (yellow, rubbery) – and also Plastic Explosives (P.E.) (made all colours, usually yellow, putty-like).

8. SAFETY RULES.

It is said that there are three stages in demolition work, (1) Scared, through lack of knowledge, (2) Careless, through over confidence and (3) Careful, after seeing an accident or having a narrow escape. A wise man goes from (1) to (3) direct. To help you we give you three safety rules: –

DON'T SMOKE NEAR EXPLOSIVES.

DON'T USE METAL INSTRUMENTS ON EXPLOSIVES (or near them where they may cause sparks).

TREAT DETONATORS VERY CAREFULLY AND KEEP THEM SEPARATE.

The reasons for each of these rules may be deduced from what has been said above.

9. Issue paper: "Explosives".

10. Stores for lecture: –

Gun Cotton	... 1 slab.	Gelignite	... 1 cartridge
T.N.T	... 1 slab.	808	... 1 cartridge
Ammonal	... 1 jar & 1 bag.	P.E.	... 2 cart's (1y. 1b.)
Picric Acid	... 1 jar.	Primer	... 1
Dynamite	... 1 cartridge.	Detonators	... 2 (1 electric)
Blasting Gelatine	... 1 cartridge.	Safety Fuse	... 4 feet.

Dec 40.

To be issued after Lecture 1

EXPLOSIVES.

SLABS.

In 1 lb. slabs, with a hole for the primer.
Packed 14 slabs in a box.
Will not detonate if wet through, but recovers if dried.
Not sensitive to rifle bullet.

(a) Gun Cotton. White fibrous slab, 6" x 3" x 1.4".
Has a small water content: if allowed to become very dry and flaky is less safe.

(b) T.N.T. Yellow brittle slab, 6" x 3" x 1.3".

POWDERS.

Of consistency of sand.
Packed in 25 lb. tins, sometimes in 4 oz. waterproof bags.
Entirely ruined by slightest damp.
Not sensitive to rifle bullets.
Best lifting or pushing explosive.

(c) Ammonal. Grey powder.

(d) Picric Acid (Melinite). Yellow powder.

(e) T.N.T. Is sometimes also made in powder form.
Yellow.

CARTRIDGES.

In 4 oz (occasionally in 2 or 8 oz) cartridges, wrapped in wax paper or cellophane.

Not damaged by water, though may decompose after several days' immersion.

Sensitive to rifle bullet (except for P.E.)

May be detonated without a primer, but if so, will usually be less effective.

All except P.E. are nitro-glycerine explosives, and are usually marked

"Arctic" or "Polar", meaning that they are still safe to handle at low temperatures. They are liable to decompose and become unsafe at high temperatures (in direct hot sun etc.) They cause headache if handled.

(f) Dynamite. Reddish-brown fudge-like substance. Not now in general use.

(g) Blasting Gelatine. Yellow jelly. Common commercial blasting explosive.

(h) Gelignite N.S. 50%. Buff, granular, putty-like substance. Common commercial explosive.

(i) 808. Yellow rubbery substance. A new explosive, and the only cartridge one which will not detonate without a primer.

(j) Plastic Explosive (P.E.). Putty-like substance, made all colours but usually yellow. Safe at all temperatures (though becomes hard if cold and melts if very hot). Withstands damp indefinitely. Not sensitive to rifle bullet. Sticks to metal with the help of vaseline or grease. May be detonated in an emergency without a primer, with no loss of power.

The best all-round explosive, but difficult and expensive to make, so supplies are limited.

Jan 41.

Practical 1
FIRING EXPLOSIVES

1. Work in three squads, with one or two instructors with each, depending on numbers. (One instructor can take up to twelve students).

2. Examine: –
   - (a) Safety fuse. 2 ft per min. Protect end from damp. Pressure increases speed.
   - (b) Detonators. Handle carefully but firmly.
     Do not bend.
   - (c) Primers. Protect from damp, especially in hole.
   - (d) Explosives. Hand round Guncotton, T.N.T., Ammonal, Gelignite and P.E.

3. Teach: –
   (a) Lighting of safety fuse. Cut fuse on long slant against boot heel. Forefinger between match and fuse.
   (b) Inserting fuse into detonator. Square end. Do not force or twist. Crimp and seal with insulating tape.
   (c) Inserting detonator into primer. Do not force or twist. Enlarge hole with wooden rectifier (or pencil) if too small. Do not push detonator in too far. Pack with grass if too loose.
   (d) Fire the charge. Danger area 50 yards.

4. Test.
   Each student to practise cutting and lighting 3" lengths of safety fuse; and to pass test of running 100 yds. over rough country, cutting and lighting three short lengths of fuse in 1½ half minutes. Start with matches and knife in pocket, fuse 100 yards distant. Each student must pass this test.

5. Practical.
   Each student to prepare and fire charge of one primer. All preparations to be done by the student himself under the instructor's eye.

6. Demonstration.
   Fire charges of one slab and 1 lb. of gelignite. Do not go into details of packing and tamping yet. Make two students fire the charges and question squad about length of fuse required.

7. Teach other methods of lighting safety fuse.
   (a) With match and longitudinal slit in fuse.
   (b) Fusee.
   (c) Match ended safety fuse.
   (d) Home-made match-ended fuse, with cellophane waterproofing.
   (e) Copper tube igniter.
   (f) Miner's igniter.
   (g) Percussion igniter.
   (h) With another fuse.

8. On conclusion, rendezvous to see: –
   (a) Electrical method of firing. Points: Ensure no shorting at joints with detonator. Sentry on battery, or keep key of exploder. Cable tied

firmly to take strain. Test power of battery or continuity of circuit with spare detonator first.
(b) Shooting at explosives. Fire rifle at gun-cotton slab, gelignite, P.E. and primer at 50 yards.

9. Stores required: –
Per squad: –

Matches, knives.		Copper tube igniters	3
Safety fuse	2 tins (96')	Miner's igniters	6
Detonators	1 tin (25)	Percussion igniters	3
Primers	2 tins (20)	Pliers	1
Insulating tape	1 reel	Crimpers	1
Gun cotton	1 lb.		
T.N.T.	1 lb.	For item 8: –	
Ammonal	¼ lb.	Gelignite	1 lb.
Gelignite	1 lb.	Primers	2
P.E.	¼ lb.	Electric detonators	3
Fusees	1 box	Cable	1 drum
Match-ended fuse	3 lengths.	Torch batteries	2
Cellophane	small piece.	Exploder	1
		Gun cotton	1 lb.
		P.E.	¼ lb.

Mar 41.

Lecture 6.
GENERAL DESTRUCTION

1. THE OBJECT.

During this course, so far, we have studied both the simple use of explosives and a few of the mechanisms used to set off explosives in laying Booby Traps. While these methods are the best for hampering the enemy war machine and lowering his morale, there are still many other ways in which one can cause him serious inconvenience.

Past experience has shown that the British Army still maintains, generally speaking, a wholesome respect for property and a complete abhorrence for doing anything in warfare except to engage the enemy in a stand up fight. This lecture is presented to you with the object of trying to break down some of these "ideals" and to develop in you the type of

mind possessed by Admiral Harwood who recently said in connection with a naval operation – "My object – DESTRUCTION."

This is a very wide subject, but in the time available it is hoped to give you some general principles and a few ideas to start the train of thought.

2. PETROL AND OILS.

In considering the destruction of any petrol and oil one must bear in mind certain essential facts.

(a) That the only practicable way is by burning. Destruction chemically can be done by lead paint, but the quantities required (about 1%) become enormous for large installations. Water and sugar have no actual effect on the petrol or oil although sugar in the petrol tank of a vehicle or water in the oil sump would cause the eventual partial destruction of the engine.

(b) That to burn petrol or oil a terrific volume of air is required and

(c) That all substances have a definite "Flash Point" (i.e. – temperature at which it will ignite).

(d) A Petrol Vapour – Air Mixture is only explosive if it contains 90 – 95 % air.

PETROL.

Bearing these in mind, let us consider petrol first and see how we can deal with the various types of Installation.

A – Above Ground Storage. These usually contain 5,000–100,000 gallons and are fitted with breather valves at the top to maintain atmospheric pressure inside. Skin is usually ⅜"–½" steel plate.

In order to get the air at the petrol the only way is to break open the side either with Anti Tank bullets or explosive 4 ozs P.E., 5" hole) and ignite by one of the following methods: –

A lighted petrol rag thrown in from upwind of the outflow; an incendiary bullet (not sure first time); and incendiary bomb or Tysule[1] placed in a shallow trench downwind and on the estimated edge of the outflow; a Verey light cartridge. If an incendiary bomb is used the charge can be fixed by Instantaneous Fuse wrapped around it. This ensures that the incendiary bomb will be burning brightly before the petrol reaches.

A special preparation of P.E./Aluminium will ignite the petrol as well as blowing in the hole.

NOTE. Tysule was a brand of capsule filled with Shell motor spirit to fill a cigarette lighter.

B – Vehicle Tanks. Same principle as in A above – a good way of disposing of vehicles. Some P.E./Aluminium mixture in a horseshoe magnet and set off with a time pencil.
C – Storage Tanks Below Ground Level. These tanks are similarly constructed but have steel stanchions and girders to hold up the 3'–5' of earth covering. They usually contain 1,000–4,000 tons.

It is a difficult matter to set fire to the petrol, the only sure way being to dig down and place explosive against the top to blow a large hole in it. This method, however, takes considerable time so the following alternatives are suggested.

Ignite the vapour at one of the two manholes and hope that the air drawn in the other manhole will eventually form an explosive mixture. This may not happen for some time and a determined man could extinguish the flame by shutting both manhole covers.

Lower a charge (30 lbs. approx.) down the manhole and explode it at the bottom. This will undoubtedly split the tank and allow the petrol to drain away.

Lower a charge (5 lbs.) tied to a cylinder of liquid Oxygen, ignite the vapour at the manhole and arrange that your incendiary bomb ignites the fuse to the charge.

Destroy intake and outlet pipes, usually contained in access tunnel, or attack the skin at the access tunnels.

For smaller installations, such as the 1,000 gallon tank under the petrol pump at a garage, the same principles apply. Introducing water into such a tank through the intake pipe by a hose will force the petrol out onto the surface where it can be ignited.

HEAVY OILS.

And now let us consider the Heavy Oils such as lubricating oil and Diesel Oils. These generally have a high Flash Point and are very difficult to ignite.

The best way known is to spread it out in the air, pour petrol over it and put down on the surface piles of rags soaked in petrol over every 20 square yards. The burning petrol will eventually raise the heat of the oil to its Flash Point.

Crude Oils – are more easily ignited as they still contain all the more volatile substances of petrol.

3. AMMUNITION.

The guiding principle to remember about ammunition is that the explosive in projectiles is H.E. and can best be destroyed by detonating it; and that the explosive in Cartridge cases is Low Explosive and merely burns rapidly.

Consequently in Shell Dumps put H.E. in amongst a pile of shells at several points and hope that the detonating wave will spread. For S.A.A. it is best to build large fires around the Dump.

4. MACHINERY.

In destroying machinery or any plant in a prearranged plan it is strongly recommended that Technical Advice should be sought to overcome any special safety devices which may exist. The following general notes may assist:

(a) Boilers – boilers are usually fitted with safety valves; find these and stop them if possible shutting all draw off files and breaking the valve controls. Then stoke up the boiler. Alternatively place some H.E. (1 lb) fitted with a detonator and match ended fuse in a lump of coal or merely in the furnace itself.

(b) Bearings – Bearings with oiling cups or oiling rings are quickly damaged by sand or silt. Otherwise blow them up.

(c) Transformers – Draw off cooling oil in outer casing. This will eventually bring about the destruction of the Transformer by overheating.

(d) Valves – any machine fitted part – know how to get at them and destroy.

(e) Drains – A 5 lb. charge down a sewer produces good results.

(f) Water Pipes – Attach special joints or casting destroy valves.

As a general rule one should attack the source of power.

5. MISCELLANEOUS DAMAGE.

Beside the above we can do temporary or permanent damage to many other things. A few examples are:

(a) Cut anchor chains on ships.

(b) Burn store houses.

(c) Blow sluice gates.

(d) Cut base of electric pylon.

(e) Attack Lock gates – either (i) deliberately by mining the wall behind the hinge or (ii) by lowering a charge of 30–50 lbs. down the wall beside the hinge and opening gate on to it.

(f) Telephone wires – earth them by fine wire along the cross trees to the earthing wire or cut them down.

(g) Aircraft – incendiarism is probably best attack; petrol tank first if possible.

6. DISLOCATION OF ENEMY EFFORT.

All the methods so far have been total direct destruction. By being more subtle one can cause a large amount of inconvenience by any of the following suggestions:

(a) Change red lights for green on railway signals.
(b) Set railway track in motion downhill.
(c) Get into railway sidings or marshalling yards and alter destination labels on trucks.
(d) Tysules in Post Boxes.
(e) Loosen rails on outside bends – place stones in railway points.

8. CONCLUSION.

In conclusion it is emphasised that it should be the aim of an Officer, N.C.O. or man to do as much destruction as is possible within the time at his disposal during a raid or during a withdrawal.

To be really effective one must make careful preparation and seek the best advice available. When doing the job be really ruthless. For instance, one would never be content with merely derailing a train; one should also try to set fire to it and place A.P. Bullets in the vicinity – covering the whole wreck by fire if it is at all possible.

The possible future use of chemical warfare provides even wider scope, but even now one can over chlorinate the enemy's water to increase his already unhappy state of mind.

Dec 40.

CHAPTER 3

MEMORANDUM ON THE ORIGINS OF THE SPECIAL AIR SERVICE

By Col. David Stirling, DSO, OBE,
8 November 1948
Selected points 7–21 inclusive

7. My written appreciation to the C-in-C (which led to the formation of "L" Detachment) was on these lines:

(a) I pointed out that the enemy was exceedingly vulnerable to attack along the line of his coastal communications and on his various transport parks, aerodromes and other targets strung out along the coast, and that the role of No. 8 Commando, which had attempted raids on these targets, was a most valuable one.

(b) I submitted that the scale on which the Commando raids had been planned, i.e., the number of bodies employed on the one hand and the scale of equipment and facilities on the other, prejudiced surprise beyond all possible compensating advantage in respect of the defensive and aggressive striking power afforded; and that, moreover, the facilities that the Navy had to provide to lift the Force resulted in the risking of Naval Units valuable out of all proportion to the maximum possible success of the raid.

(c) I argued the advantages of establishing a unit based on the principle of the fullest exploitation of surprise and of making the minimum demands on man-power and equipment. I argued that the application of this principle would mean in effect the

employment of a sub-unit of five men to cover a target previously requiring four troops of a Commando, i.e., about 200 men. I sought to prove that, if an aerodrome or transport park was the objective of an operation, then the destruction of 50 aircraft or units of transport was more easily accomplished by a sub-unit of five men than by a force of 200 men. I further concluded that 200 properly selected, trained and equipped men, organised into sub-units of five should be able to attack at least thirty different objectives at the same time on the same night as compared to only one objective using the Commando technique; and that only 25% success in the former was the equivalent to many times the maximum possible result in the latter.

The corollary of this was that a Unit operating on these principles would have to be so trained as to be capable of arriving on the scene of operation by every practical method, by land, sea or air; and that, furthermore, the facilities required for the lift must not be of a type valuable in tactical scale operations. If in any particular operation, a sub-unit was to be dropped by parachute, training must be such as to enable it to be dropped from any type of aircraft conveniently available without any modifications; if by sea, then the sub-unit must be transported either by Submarine or Caiques and trained in the use of folboats; if by land, the unit must be trained either to infiltrate on foot or be carried by the Long Range Desert Group.

(d) I insisted with the C-in-C that the Unit must be responsible for its own training and operational planning and that, therefore, the Commander of the Unit must come directly under the C-in-C. I emphasised how fatal it would be for the proposed unit to be put under any existing Branch or formation for administration. (I was determined to combat in advance any risk of being taken over by G(R), the Middle East equivalent of S.O. (E), which was already showing signs of being the monstrous and inefficient octopus it later became; or coming under the control of the Director of Combined Operations). I pointed out that the Head of any such Branch or Formation would have less experience than myself or successor in the medium in which we proposed to operate.

(e) In order to help sell the proposition, I put forward a detailed plan for the employment of the Unit in the approaching offensive (November 1941), the preparation for which was no secret.

The proposed operation (which was in fact undertaken) was, in brief, to drop by parachute five parties on the night of D minus 2 to attack the five main forward Fighter and Bomber Enemy landing grounds at Timini and Gazala. The D.Zs of these sub-units were to be some 12 miles South into the Desert from their objectives and they were to be dropped at night without moon, thus preserving surprise to the utmost. A heavy raid on the Gazala and Timini areas with the dropping of many flares was to be laid on in order to assist the aircraft carrying out the lift to establish a point on the coast line from which the navigators could have fixed line-bearing for the DZ. After re-assembling on the DZs, each party was to spend the balance of that night getting to the pre-arranged lying up place from which, the next day, they could observe their target. The following night (D minus 1 to D1), each party was to carry out its raid so as to arrive on the landing grounds at the same time. Each party was to carry a total of about 60 incendiary cum explosive bombs equipped with two hour, half hour, ten minute time pencils and also a twelve second time fuse. (Thus in the early stages of the raid a two hour time pencil was used, followed later on by the one hour and the half hour, thereby reducing the risk of the enemy removing the bombs after the warning given by the first explosion).

After the raid, the Sections were to retire into the Desert to a pre-arranged meeting place South of the Trig el Abd where a patrol of the L.R.D.G. would pick them up.

8. Having submitted these proposals to the C-in-C. I was three days later summoned to the D.C.G.S., Maj- Gen Neil Ritchie. He took me along to the C-in-C and CGS and after some discussion they agreed that the Union [unit, sic.] should be formed forthwith and that I should continue to plan the operation proposed in conjunction with the DMO. Being at that time only a Subaltern, they promoted me to Captain and gave me authority to

recruit the Unit from Layforce, and if this did not provide the number required, from certain forward formations in the Desert.

ORIGIN OF THE S.A.S. NAME

9. At the time of the Unit's formation, about the end of July 1941, Brigadier Dudley Clarke (later of "A" force) was responsible for a Branch in the Middle East which dealt among other things with enemy deception. One of his objects was to persuade the enemy that there was a fully equipped parachute and glider brigade in the Middle East. (To help delude the enemy he used to drop dummy parachutists to stimulate training exercises near POW cages and he also parked bogus gliders in the Desert hoping for photographic reconnaissance by the enemy). He called this phantom brigade the first S.A.S. Brigade.

Dudley Clarke welcomed the creation of a flesh and blood parachute unit which greatly assisted him in his game with the enemy. To humour him, we agreed to name our unit "L" Detachment, S.A.S. Brigade. Thus was the origin of the name, Special Air Service (having helped him on this, Dudley Clark gave constant assistance and help in the early days of the establishing of "L" Detachment).

RECRUITMENT

10. The original establishment passed by the War Establishment Committee for "L" Detachment was 7 Officers and about 60 ORs with a very high proportion of NCOs. The Unit was divided down into 5 troops, each of which had two Sections of 4 men and an NCO or Officer in command – the balance was made up of HQ and Camp Staff.

11. I recruited the bulk of the Unit from Layforce, which had by this time been largely disbanded. They were first class material and all of them had already had considerable operational experience and had done a good deal of night training. I also got a few men from my own Regiment, the Scots Guards, who had a Battalion in the Desert.

12. I found, during this and subsequent stages, that the A.G. Branch was unfailingly obstructive and uncooperative. Most Branches of Middle East HQ were helpful at the top level but astonishingly tiresome at the middle or lower levels. The A.G. Branch was unfortunately obstructive right up to the top and it was only by appealing to the DCGS that I could ever

have made my way. You will appreciate that it was essential for me to get the right Officers and I had a great struggle to get them. In particular I wanted Jock Lewis, who I reckoned would be the ideal Officer for the Units' training programme. I finally extricated him and he arrived a week after the Unit's formation at Kabrit.

TRAINING

13. The formation of the Unit was completed at Kabrit in early August 1941, thus allowing a period of about three months to train for the Gazala/Timini operation. The Unit, during this period, had also to be trained to operate on the general lines indicated in Paragraph 7. Jock Lewis, who was in full charge of the training, was the best training officer I have ever associated with or heard of in the War. (He was also brilliant operationally.)

14. We had to devise parachute training methods from scratch. Repeated requests to Ringway produced no assistance whatsoever. Finally, after we had lost two men in our only fatal accident throughout training, I sent a final appeal to Ringway and they sent some training notes and general information, which arrived at the end of October after the completion of our parachute training course. Included in this information, we discovered that Ringway had had a fatal accident caused by exactly the same defect as in our case. Therefore, if they had sent the information earlier, we would have undoubtedly avoided this accident. (Mention of this episode and other rather derogatory remarks in these notes are for your own information, obviously not for publication). In favour of Ringway I must add that they sent us out Captain Peter Waugh who arrived two days before the Gazala operation and he was most useful in the final preparations. Waugh stayed with us and later joined the SAS.

15. In our training programme the principle on which we worked was entirely different from that of the Commandos. A Commando unit, having once selected from a batch of volunteers, were committed to these men and had to nurse them up to the required standard. "L" Detachment, on the other hand, had set a minimum standard to which all ranks had to attain and we had to be most firm in returning to their units those who were unable to reach that standard.

16. I might also add that we insisted on the Brigade of Guards standard of discipline and smartness of turnout. There had grown up in the

Commandos a tradition that to be a tough regiment it was necessary to act tough all the time in the Barracks and on leave and they were liable to be badly dressed, ill disciplined and noisy in the streets and restaurants of Cairo. We insisted with "L" Detachment that toughness should be reserved entirely for the benefit of the enemy.

THE FIRST PARACHUTE OPERATION S.A.S. NOVEMBER 1941

17. This operation was undertaken without any modification as planned and put forward to the C-in-C in Paragraph 7.

Unfortunately the night on which it took place was almost unbelievably unsuitable for a parachute operation. There was no moon and the wind was so strong that on arriving in our Bombay aircraft over the Gazala coastline, the flares dropped by the Wellington bombers were quite insufficient for our navigators to pick up any fixed point on the coast because the Desert sand and dust was obscuring the whole coastline. Therefore, in effect, the navigators had to take pot luck in their dead reckoning and as far as I know, no party was dropped within 10 miles of the selected DZs. One of the five Bombays never dropped its stick of parachutists at all but landed the next morning on the Gazala landing ground with the whole unit still on Board. This fantastic affair was brought about by a chain of mischance. The Captain of aircraft had decided that conditions were too bad to drop his party and was, therefore, returning to his base when engine trouble occurred. He had to make a forced landing in the Desert. After the engine was repaired he radioed a request for a direction beam, which was promptly provided by the German staff on one of the Gazala landing grounds. Unsuspecting the Captain accepted the course and a little later discovered that his Bombay was being escorted by German Fighters, which forced him to put down on the main Fighter landing ground at Gazala. The fate of the four other parties was a mixed one. Two men were killed on landing, owing to the severity of conditions, and of the rest only 18 ORs and 4 Officers (Paddy Mayne, who later commanded the 1st SAS Regiment, Bill Fraser, Jock Lewis and myself) got to the LRDG rendezvous. Thus the operation was a complete failure.

SUBSEQUENT OPERATIONS

18. December 1941/March 1942

During these four months, we carried out about 20 actual raids against various targets, mostly enemy landing grounds, which the C-in-C had

laid down should be top priority. These raids included targets at Nofilia, Agheila, Buerat, Sirte (twice), Tamet (twice), Berce, Berka and Benina (twice). We destroyed about 115 aircraft and also a considerable number of enemy road transport units – we concentrated particularly on heavy diesel and petrol carrying vehicles. All these raids were carried out in conjunction with the LRDG who were able to drop us more comfortably and more accurately within striking distance of the target's area than was possible from the air. Our casualties were very light but unfortunately included Jock Lewis, who was killed by enemy bombing while returning from a raid on the Marble Arch aerodrome.

Our method of operation, apart from the means of arrival, was very much as planned for the Gazala/Timini raids.

19. April, May and June

About April, the Unit had been increased in size. "L" Detachment was recruited back to its old strength and the recruits were undergoing training. I had taken on a Unit of 60 Free French parachutists under Captain Berget, all of whom had been parachute trained at Ringway. On arriving at Kabrit they were given six weeks of intensive training in SAS methods. They were first class operatives. In addition, Captain Buck with his German speaking Unit, had joined "L" Detachment. His Unit of a dozen men consisted mostly of ex-German regular soldiers who had got out of Germany before the war for political and other reasons.

Sometime in April or May 1942, an important convoy had assembled in Alexandria. Its safe arrival in Malta was vital. "L" Detachment offered to attack on the same night the main landing grounds from which the Intelligence Branch reckoned the enemy would conduct their main efforts at straffing the convoy. The operation went reasonably well. We attacked nine landing grounds, two of which were in Crete and seven in Cyrenaica, destroying a total of about 75 aircraft and grounding a good many more over the vital period.

The two sub-units covering Crete were landed by submarine and folboat, whereas those in Cyrenaica were dropped by LRDG and picked up by them after the operation – that is, all except one party of French which arrived at their aerodrome as a party of POWs under German escort, the German escort being made up of Buck's Germans.

By the end of June, "L" Detachment had raided all the more important German and Italian aerodromes within 300 miles of the forward area at least once or twice and a few of them, even three or four times. Methods of defence were beginning to improve and although the advantage still lay with "L" Detachment, the time had come to alter our own methods. Therefore, we developed the jeep with two sets of twin Vickers K guns or alternatively one set of Vickers K guns and one Browning point 5. The astonishing agility of the jeep enabled us to approach a target at night over almost any country. The technique turned out to be most successful and enabled the Unit to be very much more flexible in its methods of operation.

By the end of July, the unit was entirely motorised – our transport consisting of jeeps and four wheeled drive 3 tonners. The LRDG had given us tremendous assistance in training a Cader [sic. cadre?] of navigators and in many other ways and we were now self-supporting.

20. <u>July to October</u>
During the period which the 8th Army stood at El Alamein, we maintained almost continuously a base between Siwa and Mersah Matruh. Originally we had established this base and supplied it by infiltrating through the El Alamein position. When this became too much of an organised line, we established a route through the Quattara Depression. Later still, when our route across the Depression was mined and patrolled by the enemy at the Cara end, we had to divert our supplies and reinforcements down the Nile and across the desert via El Kharga to the Kufra Oasis and North through the Great Sand Sea at Howards Cairn to our forward base near Siwa. Thus patrols had to detour nearly 1,800 miles to deal with an objective that might be only 40 miles from the 8th Army's forward positions.

The most important and least successful operation undertaken in this period was a large scale raid on the harbour installations and shipping at Benghazi which took place late in September. You can envisage the difficulties of supply in operating against a target as far away as Benghazi on a scale of a battalion. I lost about 50 three tonners and about 40 jeeps on this raid but fortunately not very many personnel. I had become committed to this Benghazi operation before I fully understood its implications and it was a sharp lesson which confirmed my previous views

on the error of attacking strategical targets on a tactical scale. Prior and subsequent to the Benghazi operation our main efforts from our base near Siwa had been directed against enemy landing rounds and a variety of other targets, such as drums of materials, wireless stations, coastal rest camps, transport parks, etc. We also frequently mined the main coastal road and left booby traps wherever opportunity offered. In early October we abandoned the attacking of enemy landing grounds and concentrated on the interrupting of the enemy supply system, particularly their Desert railway line.

21. Mid October to January 1943
After Rommell's route to El Alamein, General Montgomery instructed us to continue our concentration exclusively on the enemy's communications. During late November when Rommell was making an apparently determined effort to stabilise his position in the Agheila area, we were able to contribute quite importantly to Rommell's difficulties. On previous campaigns it had been at Agheila that the supply position usually began to swing in favour of the enemy.

We undertook at this stage to maintain continuously a patrol covering off over a 40 mile section of the enemy's coastal communications from Tripoli to Marble Arch. This required the establishing and supplying of 16 sub-bases from which 16 patrols could operate against the coastal communications at least twice or three times a week each within their own allocated 40 mile sectors. This meant a minimum of about three to four raids every night somewhere on the enemy's main coast communication between Tripoli and Agheila. In practice the operation went very successfully east of and including the Buerat area. North of Wadi Zem the country was very much more difficult for operations due to its dense population, and the SAS patrols although very successful to start off with, were mostly driven off or rounded up after three weeks. However, we certainly succeeded in stopping enemy tpt movement by night for a considerable period, thus forcing transport movement by day which provided the RAF with good straffing targets. By the middle of January we had shifted our activities westwards and were mounting patrols and continued raiding on enemy communications as far north as Sfax in Tunisia (incidentally this is where I was captured by a German Reconnaissance Unit).

CHAPTER 4

SECRET AND PERSONAL LETTER TO THE PRIME MINISTER FROM MAJOR RANDOLPH S. CHURCHILL

June 1942

Mid-East

June 24, 1942. I have obtained the permission of my C.O. David Stirling, to send you an account of the operation upon which I recently accompanied him, and returning from which I was involved in the car accident which has landed me in hospital. The expedition on which we set out – owing to a number of accidents – proved fruitless, but it had a certain reconnaissance value, and as it was the first I had been on, I found it extremely exciting.

Our object was to sink two enemy ships in Benghazi in such a way as to block the channel to the harbour. The plans had been made and rehearsed before I joined the unit, and I only accompanied the party to study the technique of the Long Range Desert Group whose job it was to take us about 25 miles short of Benghazi. The party which was to undertake the operation consisted of six, and I was only a "spare file". But David promised me if anything happened to any of the six, I should be allowed to go the whole way.

Our own car was a Ford utility car stripped down to look like a German staff car. We first drove under our own steam to Siwa; there we joined forces with the L.R.D.G. patrol consisting of five trucks. From here we drove about 400 miles, taking four days over the trip. We halted under good cover some 50 miles from Benghazi, and it was here that one of the corporals, while preparing explosives, had an accident with a detonator which injured his hand; and providentially for me, only two hours before they were due to take off on the last lap it secured me a seat in the Ford.

As soon as it was dark, we set off with two trucks from the L.R.D.G. to

guide us. About 11 that night they landed us on the road about 25 miles each [sic] of Benghazi. We hit the road within half a mile of where we wanted, which was a very creditable bit of navigation on the part of the L.R.D.G. after a journey of 400 miles.

All went well until we reached the fine concrete road about 10 miles outside the town. A screeching noise like a car cornering at very high speed then began, and persisted however slowly we drove. We stopped to try and put it right, but our efforts were unavailing, and we eventually discovered that, during our long approach march, our front wheels had come out of alignment and in addition our front axle had got bent. So there was nothing for it but to go on, though the noise was frightful and could be heard half a mile away. But the main harm it did was, I think, to our own nerves, as we already had somewhat guilty consciences about what we planned to do and we did not like the idea of attracting so much attention.

We knew our first obstacle would be a road block three miles outside the town; and we hoped to get through this profiting by the linguistic ability of Fitzroy Maclean. He was sitting in the front of the car. David Stirling was driving, and between them was Gordon Alston who knew Benghazi well as he was there for three weeks during the last occupation. I sat in the middle at the back, with the sergeant on one hand and the corporal on the other, whose duty it was to get out and silently clock the sentries if they failed to yield to Fitzroy's blandishments. We were not going to fire if it could possibly be avoided, but all of us in the back had Tommy guns and several handfuls of grenades.

The guard was alert and well placed. The sentry who challenged us remained about five yards beyond us to the right, while his colleague was about 25 yards away to the left. Both of them pointed fixed bayonets at us while another three of their colleagues stayed in the background. It looked as if it would be impossible to dispose of them silently. Fortunately, however, when Fitzroy summoned the right-hand sentry to the car and answered his challenge with the single word "Militaire", he merely reproved us for showing too much light and stood aside, as we drove on with a distinct feeling of elation coupled with relief.

We could not dim our lights any further so we turned them out – luckily there was still another half-hour of moon left so we could see all right.

We saw no one until we came to the centre of the town, when a car came towards us and after it had gone about 100 yards turned round and with another car came after us. They seemed to be gaining on us, and although David accelerated they still seemed to be gaining. Having no lights and making this frightful screeching noise, we already thought we were detected, when suddenly off went a siren. We knew that the R.A.F. were not going to bomb Benghazi that night, though they had been over the three previous nights, so it looked as if we had walked straight into a trap. We crammed on our full speed, getting up to 80 m.p.h. and, relying on Gordon Alston's local knowledge, David by superb driving suddenly crammed on the brakes and shot round a corner into a narrow street and drove on about 500 yards into the native part of the town, where we stopped and awaited developments. Police whistles sounded all over the town, and soon cars were roaring about at top speed. It looked as if we were properly "in the bag". It was clear we could not hope to get out in our car which, in gangster parlance, was "hot". So David gave an order for a half-hour time pencil to be put in the car which, as it was chock-full of thermite and plastic, would go off with a pretty detonation.

It seemed our only chance was to get out on foot so, the fuse being set, we legged it through the Arab town, which had been badly knocked about by bombing and which is deserted by night as the Arabs all sleep outside the town. We found a ruined house and there we waited. After about ten minutes we thought we did not want the car (which I forgot to say we had backed into a side alley) to go off while we were still in the neighbourhood, so we changed the half-hour pencil for a two-hour one. Unfortunately the corporal forgot to deal satisfactorily with the discarded detonator which, ten minutes later, went off with what seemed to us an enormous bang.

After about a quarter of an hour another siren went off and quiet began to descend on the town, so Fitzroy and David went back to make a reconnaissance. Fitzroy walked up to the first sentry he saw and asked him in Italian what was going on. He said it was a false air-raid alarm; so it appeared our fears had been groundless and that the excitement and alarm had nothing whatever to do with us.

Looking back in retrospect, we were perhaps foolish to assume we were the cause of it, but so many circumstances taken together – having no lights, the screeching of our tyres, the sirens and whistles, the supposed pursuit by two cars – all conspired to mislead us, and in combination certainly gave me the most exciting half-hour of my life.

We then decided to get on and do the job, but what with the false alarm and the halt in the road trying to mend the car we had lost about one-and-a-half hours of valuable time, and whereas we had intended to

inflate two rubber boats we now decided there was only time for one.

I was left on guard over the car, which the sergeant had another shot at repairing. He got down underneath it with a torch while I kept watch. Five or six times people passed on their way to and from the docks, and we had to suspend work and lie doggo. Meanwhile, the other four carried the boat and explosives down to the dock, which was about 500 yards away. There was no time to make a proper reconnaissance, or try to sneak through the barbed wire which surrounds it without being perceived by sentries, so Fitzroy marched up to a sentry and said in Italian he was a German officer, and demanded permission to enter which was at once accorded. They then set to work blowing up the boat and sorting out their explosives, only to discover a vital fuse must have been dropped on their way down to the dock. David went off to get another. Meanwhile Fitzroy was pumping away with his bellows only to discover, after some ten minutes, that the boat was punctured.

By now the look-outs on the various ships in the harbour kept challenging him; he replied he was a German officer and, eventually that he was very bored with being challenged and they were to shut up, which for the moment they did.

The boat being punctured, there was nothing for it but to put it in its huge kit-bag and bring it back to the car. Unfortunately, Fitzroy passed David en route without recognising him, and David on his return to the dock had some difficulty in getting past the sentry, but mumbling incoherently and pushing him aside he walked straight in. Fitzroy collected the second boat from the car, lugged it down to the dock, where he and David started blowing it up.

Meanwhile Gordon had been making a reconnaissance of the dock area, and on arriving back had some difficulty with the sentry. Fitzroy went off to adjust the matter, but it seemed by this time the sentry was getting suspicious and he prodded Fitzroy in the stomach with his bayonet, and now the challenges from the ships in the harbour had begun to be renewed. It was quite clear that although they might be allowed to blow up the boat on the quayside, they would hardly be allowed to launch it and row out into the harbour and fix their limpets to the side of the ships.

By this time 20 or 30 people were watching, so Fitzroy angrily said to the sentry: "Who is in charge of this guard?" The sentry, pointing to a tent, said a corporal in it was in charge. Whereupon Fitzroy instructed him to turn out his guard, and proceeded to give them all a terrific dressing down.

He said (in Italian), "We are German officers and we have come here to test your security arrangements". They are appalling. We have been past this sentry four or five times. He has not asked us once for our identity cards. For all he knows, we might be English. We have brought great bags into the dock. How is he to know they are not full of explosives? It is a very bad show indeed. We have brought all this stuff in here, and now we are going to take it out again".

This they then proceeded to do, and they were smartly saluted by the corporal as they went.

David meanwhile had told me that he was pretty sure he would not be able to do any good that night, and that I must find a place where we could hide the car and lie up until the following night.

I found a private garage which had been knocked about by bombing. Unfortunately the street was so very narrow the driver had to drive the car back and forwards about 25 times (making the most frightful noise) before it was discovered the entrance was a quarter of an inch too small. Eventually we discovered another similar place, and after a good deal of shunting got the car in.

All this took a great deal of time and was rather alarming, as I did not know how I would fare if anyone came along and asked me what I was doing.

Now it was light, and we all ascended to the house on top of the garage and went to sleep. We woke about 7 o'clock in very high spirits and feeling there was nothing we could not get away with inside Benghazi. Suddenly, however, the whole town became alive. We did not realise that though the Arabs sleep outside the town they all return to their houses during the day. The staircase in our house was in a patio which shared a common wall with the house next door, which had a similar patio to our own. Into this soon came an aged Arab couple who pattered about preparing their breakfast.

This compelled us to keep extremely quiet and talk in nothing but whispers. (I found this extremely difficult) I also exposed us to the fear that the owner of the house might return though its incredible state of filth made us feel it had been evacuated. So it proved, but the day was long and very trying. We only had about two books between us – I luckily had F.S. Oliver's "Alexander Hamilton".

We took it in turns to keep watch, and had decided if anyone should come in our best chance was to have Fitzroy engage him in conversation, then seize him and tie him up.

I was keeping watch about 4 o'clock when I heard someone coming up the stairs very noisily. I thought it was the sergeant who had gone down some time before to work on the car, but on looking round the corner to my horror I saw it was an Italian sailor. I darted back to get Fitzroy, but apparently the sailor had seen me and terrified by my appearance (I had quite a long beard which I am sure you would not have liked), he fell headlong down the stairs and bolted out before our two soldiers in the garage could catch him. (I should have explained there were two or three entrances to the house).

This threw us all into a considerable state of alarm, but on thinking it over it seemed most unlikely the sailor had come there looking for us, or that his fleeting glimpse of me would make him guess that in the house there were six fully armed British soldiers together with a car. It seemed most likely he had come there looting, and finding the house occupied, had cleared out in a panic. Whatever the explanation, we lay there unmolested, but from now on every sound in the street filled us with apprehension.

We knew the R.A.F. were going to bomb the town that night, so it was decided to have another shot at the ships under cover of the air-raid. About 10–30 the harbour party sailed out to make a reconnaissance, and on reaching the harbour found that there was a ship of about 3000 tons on fire, which lit up the whole harbour area. No bombs had been dropped, and we still do not know what caused the fire.

The light it gave out was a tremendous handicap to our operation, and as an additional disappointment the all-clear sounded almost immediately.

We subsequently discovered that the R.A.F., seeing the fire, thought we had caused it and thought they had better not interfere, so went off to drop their bombs on neighbouring aerodromes.

It was clearly impossible to launch a boat, as there were squads of people standing around to watch the fire and everything was clearly illumined. David considered the desirability of putting delayed action charges in three M.T.B.s which were right alongside the quay but eventually decided it was not worth while giving away the fact we had been inside Benghazi for so small a prize, as we now felt that we could easily return later and make a proper job of the ships. So he decided instead we would go off and attack our second objective, which was Benina aerodrome.

The men had been working all day on the car, and we hoped now it would make less noise. Unfortunately, as soon as we got to the main road the noise was as bad as ever; so we stopped – this time in one of the main streets of Benghazi – and had another shot at putting it right.

We went to work for about one and a half hours, and during this time many people passed us, but of course nothing arouses less sensation than people working on a car, and nobody challenged us, no doubt for fear of being asked to give a hand! In fact no one said a word to us, and we worked on as hard as we could.

All, however, to no avail. The car still made as much noise as ever. It was now about 3 o'clock, and we had to get going. There was still time to have beaten up Benina, but the noise our car made might have made escape impossible and would have revealed the fact that we had been inside Benghazi, for our screechings inside Benghazi and at Benina would plainly have been associated once we did anything to provoke enquiry. So there was nothing for it but to go back to breakfast with the L.R.D.G.

We had to negotiate the road block once more. This time they were a little more inquisitive, and upon Fitzroy shouting "Militaire" they enquired "What sort of militaire"?, to which Fitzroy responded "German Staff Officers", and the sentry replied "Molto Bene".

It was very disappointing that we failed to achieve anything. On the other hand, it has filled us with confidence for future operations of a similar kind. Fitzroy of course is worth his weight in gold. He speaks German and Italian almost perfectly, in addition to French and Russian. With him at my side I would be perfectly happy to spend a week in Rome.

Our return journey was wholly uneventful except we picked up a couple of Senussis who belonged to the Senussi battalion which got left behind in the retreat in January.

It was on the very last lap that we had the car smash. It was at night, and we were driving from Alexandria to Cairo. We had gone about 30 miles, and were passing a long convoy of trucks coming towards us. Suddenly the last one pulled out right in front of us. David swerved sharply off the road, but it just touched our near rear wheel and swung us broadside across the road. Our car turned over a couple of times. All of us fortunately were thrown clear, excepting Arthur Merton, the Daily Telegraph war correspondent, whom we had met in Alexandria and to whom we were giving a lift. He was pinned in the car. He had a number of fractures in the head and unfortunately died before he got to hospital. We were all picked up quite quickly and taken back to Alexandria.

Gordon Alston, Fitzroy, the Sergeant and myself all had fairly serious injuries, but David, as always, had the luck of the devil, and was wholly

unscathed. He left us next morning to go off on another similar enterprise. He is now a few days overdue, but I feel sure he will turn up quite all right.

I should explain that L. Detachment is not primarily concerned with parachuting. It is a long range specialized sabotage unit. We learn to parachute in case that is the best method of reaching the target. But more often we use the L.R.D.G. or submarines.

June, 26, 1942. David has just got back safe and sound. He burnt down 3 hangars at Benina Aerodrome, destroying about 14 aero engines, 4 aircraft, and all the aero-engine workshops.

We waited till the first delayed-action charge went up and then opened the door of the guard-house. Inside, facing him, was a German officer seated at a table with about 15 German soldiers drawn up in front of him. David opened his hand and showed the Hun officer a hand grenade. The Hun wailed "No – no – no!" "Yes – yes – yes!" replied David lobbing it in and closing the door. There was a fine bang and as he made off into the darkness a few low moans was all that could be heard from the guard-house.

David then hid for three days, and then returned and shot up a lot of enemy transport about 4 miles outside Benghazi. He had twin mounted Vickers K. guns on a big truck and destroyed about 15 large lorries, killing another 10 Huns. He then drove off and made good his escape up the escarpment.

The severe jolting going up the escarpment caused a time pencil to break. The corporal at the back yelled "Abandon truck". They all jumped out and had got about 30 yards when the truck which had 50 lbs. of plastic in it, went sky high.

I forgot to mention that on the approach march between Siwa and Benghazi David drove his car on to a thermos bomb. The car was finished but all the occupants O.K. except for the shaking. Never a dull moment!

CHAPTER 5

"TOUGHEST JOB IN THE WAR"

by Gordon Gaskill, *The American Magazine*, July 1942
By cable from Cairo

Our Middle East correspondent goes parachuting with Britain's new super-commandos ... and brings back the first story of the "fighting fools" of the desert.

Here, for the first time, the veil of military censorship is lifted from one of the newest, most effective striking forces in this war. Gordon Gaskill, our young correspondent who reported the first bombing attack on American ships at Suez, who rode with the British in tanks and low-flying fighting planes over the Libyan battlefield, now gives to the world the first close-up glimpse of the daring British parachute commandos in action. He followed them into the desert and saw the terror and havoc they spread among the enemy. – THE EDITOR.

THE Italian commandant was frantic. The world had gone mad tonight. He couldn't believe his eyes, still fogged by sleep, for it was three o'clock in the morning. His airdrome garrison town seemed to be under heavy attack and half of it was already blazing.

His bewildered brain told him that it was impossible. The damned British were at least 250 miles away, no planes have been sighted, and surely they couldn't ... The gasoline dumps went up with a mighty roar. One by one a line of airplanes began exploding into flames, apparently by themselves.

The commandant almost sobbed; the planes had been brand-new.

He cursed his 800 troops, now running about wild and witless. They carried rifles and submachineguns, but had no targets. So they fired everywhere – at anything – at everything – at nothing. Ghosts and devils were abroad tonight. The commandant saw that his precious 800 were in complete panic.

So was he. He rushed a message to the next garrison: "Under heavy attack. Must have immediate help. Unable to hold out much longer."

Crouching in the wadi at the edge of the airdrome, peering happily through the desert scrub at the havoc they had caused, were the attacking British forces. Neither ghosts nor devils, they consisted of exactly two men – a young Scottish major and a cockney sergeant. They belonged to a little-known fighting group which, for bold imagination and suicidal courage, cannot be excelled anywhere on earth – British parachute troops of the Middle East.

The attack, so terrible and supernatural to the Italians, seemed quite simple to them. They had merely tiptoed about the airdrome in the dead of night depositing little 16-ounce delayed-action bombs here and there, in any likely place – in gasoline stores, airplane cockpits, bomb piles. Then they had crept away in the darkness to hide. The major produced a flask of whisky, and they sipped it as the minutes passed. It would take 30 minutes for the bombs to begin exploding. They had plenty of time to get away later. They wanted to see the fun.

Little has been said or written about the Middle East's parachute troops. For one thing, they're an extraordinarily close-mouthed lot. Fortunately, I got to know them pretty well. I visited them several times in the little patch of desert where they train. Once I made a parachute jump with them and they liked that.

Furthermore, military censorship has pulled a curtain over their activities. An unlucky accident has now permitted that curtain to be partially lifted. A German fighter plane happened to discover a great plane full of paratroops en route to a job and riddled it with bullets. The co-pilot and the radio operator were killed, and everybody else was wounded. The pilot somehow managed to land the plane safely, but all of them were captured, with all of the equipment which the wounded men were unable to destroy. So, since the Germans now know about them, there's no reason why the whole world shouldn't.

THE young Scottish major, who so thoughtfully brought the whisky along, is responsible for the formation of the Mid-East paratroops. He is a tall, thin, and rather languid-looking aristocrat. A lowly subaltern when he arrived in the Mid-East some months ago with the famous commandos, he had a burning idea: From the commandos, which already were a picked group, he wanted to choose an even more carefully picked group, the cream of the cream, and organize them into a small, supertrained squad, capable of going anywhere, even by parachute, and doing anything. In one way or another he pushed the idea before an imaginative general, who told him to go ahead. He picked a few fellow commandos and disappeared into the desert for training.

Today, at 25, the erstwhile subaltern is one of the youngest majors in the British Army and his command has become fantastically daring, an exquisitely trained pack of killers, thieves, and saboteurs – all in a good cause. The British Army of the Nile admiringly calls them, "Bloody fools," arguing that nobody else would be mad enough to operate as much as 600 miles inside the enemy lines.

Commandos are super-soldiers, while the Mid-East's paratroops are super-commandos. Their training and equipment have been thought out to the minutest details. Even things which seem far-fetched and ridiculous have proved their worth in battle.

Once returning from a raid on foot, a body of paratroops were spotted by a Messerschmitt, which darted down to machine-gun them. They were in perfectly flat desert with no place to hide. Each man brought out a bit of burlap, dug a shallow hole in the sand, pulled the burlap over him, sprinkled sand on top, and crawled in. As far as the Messerschmitt was concerned, they simply disappeared.

Another returning party had only one quart of water for five men. They almost died of thirst until they reached the sea. Here they hooked together two water bottles with thirty-inch rubber tubing which each man carries, boiled salt water in the first bottle, and condensed fresh water in the second. It took five hours to make one quart, but it saved their lives.

The paratroops have their own special bomb. It looks like a handful of soft, black putty and can be molded into any shape, as it never hardens. It can be fused to go off instantly, or in any desired time up to 2½ hours. It is a combination of high explosive and thermite. The first blows things up, while the second sets anything, even metal, afire. It weighs only one pound, and each man easily carries at least a dozen.

The paratroops have had extraordinary luck. As a hulking Irish lieutenant put it, "The little people must watch over us." Once while sneaking away from an enemy airdrome after laying their eggs, they suddenly saw an enemy truck driving toward them with blazing headlights. In a few seconds the lights would have picked them out plainly. Just then one of their own bombs exploded back on the airdrome and the enemy driver, thinking there was an air raid on, instantly doused his lights and swept by, without seeing them.

Other incidents which appear to be nothing but luck are really something more. Like the time when the paratroops were creeping along an enemy building in the darkness. Suddenly a window above them opened and an Italian looked out. They were plainly visible in the light flooding down on them. One paratrooper pointed a tommy gun at the Italian but didn't fire. The Italian muttered something and closed the window. A British officer who understood Italian explained later: The man had thought they were his own blackout patrol and had apologized for letting so much light show! This is not luck; it is the very basis of paratroop theory. As the major explained it to me, "The enemy never expects you in his own back yard and you can move about freely, and you even have trouble convincing him that you are an enemy. I know it sounds hairbrained but it's true."

Incredible or not, it works. One night a few paratroops went to sleep in what they thought was the empty desert. In the morning when they awoke they found themselves smack in the middle of a German encampment, not fifty paces from the German colonel's tent. Their first thought was of trying to sneak away, but it was broad daylight and the ground was bare. So they packed up calmly and strolled off. They walked straight through the German camp dressed in British uniforms and nobody paid any attention to them.

IT SOUNDS strange, but sometimes parachute troops don't use parachutes.

In the desert, which is like the ocean, it's possible to drive almost anywhere with a truck without being spotted if you make wide detours and drive the ticklish stretches by night. Thus paratroops often fall in line with a moving enemy convoy at tonight. They soon learn the headlight recognition signals and blink as cheerfully as any Jerry. They park in enemy parking lots. If they need food, water, or gasoline, they merely cut one enemy truck out of the convoy or encampment and hold it up.

The primary object of the paratroop raids is to destroy vital enemy equipment and spread panic, but often they run across a large mess building or tent in the dark and can't resist the temptation to have a go at it. Their technique is now terrible and classic. "We just act as if we belong there," a lieutenant said in telling me about a raid he made with a cockney private. "We were walking across this airdrome when we saw a big building. Little cracks of lights were leaking out and inside we could hear Germans singing and talking. We didn't say a word but began walking toward the building. The private had a tommy gun with two extra magazines and I had a .45 and two extra clips. As we got nearer we realized there were a lot of men inside and the cockney private whispered, "Oh, lovely," and we damned near burst out laughing. I yanked the door open and we both began firing. I'll never forget the looks on their faces. They simply stared. Not a single person ever fired back. I suppose we killed about 50, mostly officers. I remember the cockney yelling as we ran away, "That's for London, you bloody so-and-so's!"

SO FAR the paratroops have operated only with handfuls of men; no more than 10 have ever gone out on a raid. They believe 10 can do nearly as much vital damage as 200 and run much less risk of detection, and they prefer 5 to 10 – "five good men." One captain told me firmly, "I can get in anywhere, I don't care where, I don't care how well guarded, I don't care how many sentries." I know a lieutenant who took 4 men on a raid to an important enemy drome and destroyed 24 planes in one night. Nine nights later he did exactly the same thing at exactly the same airdrome and got 27 more, a total of 51 planes in 9 days. Another group of 5 men burned up 37 planes in one night for the largest single bag. In each case, all got back safely by disappearing into the trackless desert in the darkness and later rendezvousing with trucks.

Some have lain as long as three days and nights beside enemy airdromes noting vital targets and watching in amusement the enemy taking anti-paratroop precautions every evening. Sometimes the Italians have put out so many sentries they could almost join hands, and other times stationed sentries at each plane, all to no avail. Paratroops get in anyway.

A sergeant took me under his wing when I made a thousand-foot practice jump with them. I climbed into a converted bomber with fourteen others, and like them wore a crash helmet and coverall uniform, heavy high-laced boots, and knee protectors. As we circled up to a thousand feet the sergeant kept explaining how to try to land in a relaxed half-sitting position and not worry if another parachute drifted into me. "They just kiss and float apart like two ruddy balloons," he explained.

A red "get-ready" light winked and he showed me how to hook one end of my parachute cord onto a ring which slid on a greased steel rod running lengthwise down the cabin.

Then a green light flashed and the lieutenant in command went first. The men jumped faster than one per second and I went leaping out the door before I realized it. The line tied to the plane dragged the chute from the pack, then when my full weight hit the extended line, the connection broke and I fell free. There was no sharp jerk. It was the most exhilarating sensation I've ever known as I apparently hung motionless in heaven in great silence. It was so still I could talk in almost conversational tones to other men drifting down around me.

I began swinging like a pendulum. Then the sergeant said, "Here comes the ground." Previously I felt as if I were standing still, but now suddenly the ground came into focus, rushing up at terrific speed. Actually we were dropping seventeen feet per second and it took only sixty seconds to reach the ground. I was swinging widely as I struck and tumbled head over heels twice. The chute began dragging me. I dimly remembered some advice about this, and finally recalled that there was a release knob on my chest. I turned it and the chute fell away. Then I sat down. It had been a hard jolt but I was unhurt. I ran my hands into soft, warm sand, and I felt very good.

A PRACTICE jump like that is one thing; a battle jump is quite another. That day was perfectly clear and the spot was chosen especially because the sand was the softest. You knew what you were jumping into and when you would hit, but on the first battle jump the paratroops made, it was one of the most devilish nights North Africa has known. Rain was splashing down in icy sheets in total darkness. Even on the ground the wind was a thirty-mile gale, murderous to parachutists. It was the worst possible night, but paratroops had orders to jump at all costs, so they did.

The sergeant who had taught me to jump was lost that night. The last ever seen of him was a dim shape leaping out into that shrieking darkness, not knowing what he was jumping into, not knowing when he would hit the ground.

I can think of no greater courage. On their caps the paratroops wear a winged dagger with the words, "Who dares, wins."

They are doing both.

CHAPTER 6

MEMORANDUM BY CAPT. GEORGE JELLICOE, SPECIAL AIR SERVICE

1 January 1943

I consider the Mediterranean Basin offers the fullest scope for small scale raiding that has existed in any theatre of war since September 1939. This applies particularly to the Eastern Mediterranean.

Introductory.

2. For example, in Jugoslavia and Greece alone 48 full Axis Divisions are at this moment fully occupied by fierce but often mutually inconsistent partisan activities. In Greece particularly, it is known that those bands are usually ill-armed and ill-organized. From my own observation in Crete I know how ineffective their activities for the most part are. And yet the Axis is forced to deploy at least three times as many divisions in the Balkans as in the whole of North Africa.

3. These partisan activities have as yet received little direct military encouragement or support. I am quite certain that were this support and encouragement forthcoming on a large and tangible scale the already great strain which the holding down of the Balkans entails upon the Axis resources of military manpower would become intolerable.

4. More especially if the maximum effort was timed to precede or synchronise with large scale operations in the Western Mediterranean it would have an important diversionary value.

5. The type of operation envisaged would be the simultaneous "strike" of 100 small parties previously injected by all available methods into the Balkans or the Greek Islands. The results which would be confidently anticipated have already been shown on a small scale in the synchronised

attacks on L.G.s. carried out by 1 S.A.S. Regiment in West Africa and the Greek Islands. Targets are not lacking as the recent attack on the Gorgo Potimus Bridge, resulting in the interruption of railway communications between Salonika and Athens, during a minimum of four months, shows.

Proposals.

There are at the moment certain obstacles to the full realisation of this and similar projects.

1. 1 S.A.S. Regiment has not a sufficiently sound rear organisation to provide an effective 'follow-up' to operations on the scale suggested.

Unless this rear organisation is provided at once the opportunity will be forfeited as the experience of Small Scale Raiding on the French Coast, shows.

I therefore submit the following proposal:—

"That a Rear Headquarters be established at Combined Operations Headquarters to deal with the consolidated long term administrative requirements of No. 62 Commando and 1 S.A.S. Regiment.

As regards 1 S.A.S. Regiment this Headquarters will be responsible for:-

(a) The meeting of 50% of its requirements in personnel, both officers and men, specialist and non-specialist.

(b) The provision of specialist stores of ALL types. These will include all and any specialist equipment from M.T.Bs. and Welman craft to Seasickness Tablets, the lack of which would result in a loss of operational efficiency or in an inability to exploit all available operational opportunities.

(c) The pooling and recording of all knowledge and experience, training, technical and operational. This I consider to be most important. For example it is clear to me that in certain technical respects 1 S.A.S. Regiment are 18 months out of date.

2. Much time will be lost and much friction caused unless small scale

raiding is organised on the same basis and in intimate co-operation in both the West and the East Mediterranean.

I do not consider 1 S.A.S. Regiment as at present constituted capable of covering the whole Mediterranean Basin.

I feel that the ideal solution would be the constitution of a small Advance Headquarters to be responsible for the direction of all S.S. Raiding in the Mediterranean. As this however depends on the unlikely establishment of a unified military command in North Africa I make the following proposals:—

(a) That small scale raiding in the Mediterranean should connote all aggressive military action irrespective of the means employed between but excluding the activities of the single agent and the large scale combined operation.

(b) That 1 S.A.S. Regiment with attached American personnel should undertake all small scale raiding in the Eastern Mediterranean under the operational control of the local C. in C.

(c) That a similar Force (No. 62 Commando with attached American personnel) should undertake all Small Scale Raiding in the Western Mediterranean under the operational control of the local C. in C.

(d) That a provisional but fluid line of demarcation should be agreed upon by the local C. in C.'s and the Force Commanders involved.

(e) That to secure maximum Small Scale Raiding efforts in the Eastern or Western Mediterranean as occasion demands, the personnel of both Raiding Forces should be freely interchangeable.

1.1.43.

CHAPTER 7

¼-TON 4x4 TRUCK (WILLYS-OVERLAND MODEL MB AND FORD MODEL GPW)

War Department Technical Manual TM 9-803,

February 1944

PART ONE—OPERATING INSTRUCTIONS

Figure 1—1/4-Ton 4 x 4 Truck—Left Front

Figure 2—1/4-Ton 4 x 4 Truck—Right Rear

Figure 3—1/4-Ton 4 x 4 Truck—Right Side

Figure 4—1/4-Ton 4 x 4 Truck—Right Front

Section II

DESCRIPTION AND TABULATED DATA

2. DESCRIPTION

a. Type. This vehicle is a general purpose, personnel, or cargo carrier especially adaptable for reconnaisance or command, and designated as ¼-ton 4 x 4 Truck. It is a four-wheel vehicle with four-wheel drive. The engine is a 4-cylinder gasoline unit located in the conventional place, under the hood at the front of the vehicle. A conventional three-speed transmission equipped with a transfer case provides additional speeds for traversing difficult terrain. The body is of the open type with an open driver's compartment. The folding top can be removed and stowed; and, the windshield tilted forward on top of the hood, or opened upward and outward. A spare wheel equipped with a tire is mounted on the rear of the body, and a pintle hook is provided to haul trailed loads. Specifications of the vehicle are given under "Data" (par. 3). General physical characteristics are shown in figures 1 through 4.

3. DATA

a. Vehicle Specifications.

Wheelbase	80 in.
Length, over-all	132¼ in.
Width, over-all	62 in.
Height, over-all—top up	69¾ in.
—top down	52 in.
Wheel size	combat 16 x 4.50 E.
Tire size	16 x 6.o0 in.
Tire pressure (front and rear)	35 lb.
Tire type	mud and snow
Tire plies	6
Tread (center-to-center)—front	49 in.
—rear	49 in.
Crew, operating	2
Passenger capacity including crew	5

DESCRIPTION AND TABULATED DATA

Weights:	
Road, including gas and water	2,453 lb
Gross (loaded)	3,253 lb
Shipping (less water and fuel)	2,337 lb
Boxed gross	3,062 lb
Maximum pay load	800 lb
Maximum trailed load	1,000 lb
Ground clearance	8¾ in.
Pintle height (loaded)	21 in.
Kind and grade of fuel (octane rating) Gasoline	(68 mm)
Approach angle	45 deg
Departure angle	35 deg
Shipping dimensions—cubic feet	331
—square feet	57

b. Performance.

Maximum allowable speeds (mph) with transfer case in "HIGH" range:

High gear (3rd)	65
Intermediate gear (2nd)	41
Low gear (1st)	24
Reverse gear	18

Maximum allowable speeds (mph) with transfer case in "LOW" range:

High gear (3rd)	33
Intermediate gear (2nd)	21
Low gear (1st)	12
Reverse gear	9
Maximum grade ability	(percent) 60
Minimum turning radius—right	17½ ft
—left	17½ ft
Maximum fording depth	21 in.
Towing facilities—front	none
—rear	pintle hook
Maximum draw-bar pull	1,930 lb
Engine idle speed	600 rpm
Miles per gallon—(high gear—high range)	
average conditions	20
Cruising range—(miles) average conditions	285

c. Capacities.

Engine crankcase capacity—dry	5 qt
—refill	4 qt
Transmission capacity	¾ qt
Transfer case capacity	1½ qt
Front axle capacity (differential)	1¼ qt
Rear axle capacity (differential)	1¼ qt
Front axle steering knuckle universal joint	¼ qt
Steering gear housing	¼ qt
Air cleaner (oil bath)	⅝ qt
Fuel tank capacity	15 gal
Cooling system capacity	11 qt
Brake system (hydraulic brake fluid)	¼ qt
Shock absorbers—front	5 oz
—rear	5¾ oz

d. Communications.

(1) Radio Outlet Box. A radio outlet box is provided on the later vehicles to use the vehicle battery (6-volt current supply). This outlet is located against the body side panel at the right front seat.

(2) Auxilary Generator. A 12-volt, 55-ampere auxiliary generator is furnished on some vehicles. The generator is driven by a V-belt from

a power take-off unit on the rear of the transfer case. Instructions for operation and care accompany those vehicles.

Section III
DRIVING CONTROLS AND OPERATION

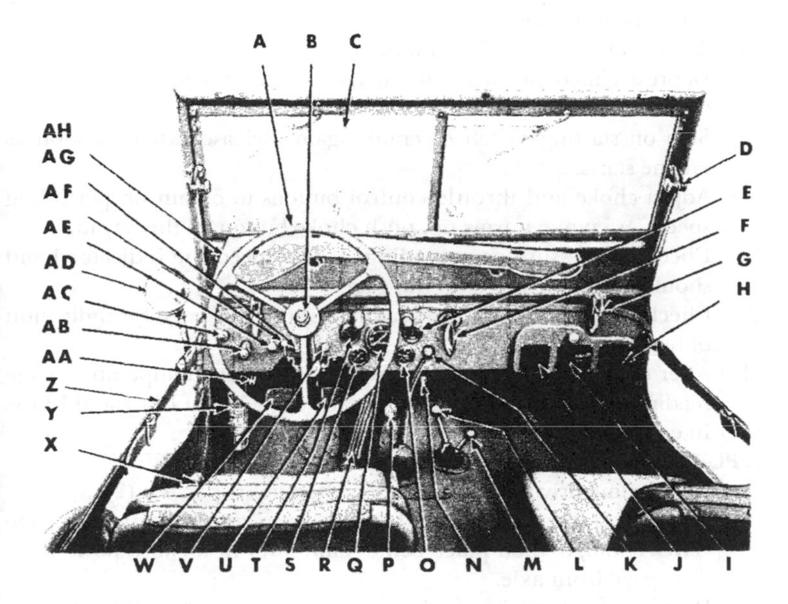

A STEERING WHEEL
B HORN BUTTON
C WINDSHIELD WIPERS
D WINDSHIELD ADJUSTING ARMS
E AMMETER
F HAND BRAKE
G WINDSHIELD CLAMPS
H CAUTION PLATE
I NAME PLATE
J SHIFT PLATE
K TRANSMISSION GEAR SHIFT LEVER
L TRANSFER CASE SHIFT LEVER—FRONT AXLE DRIVE
M TRANSFER CASE SHIFT LEVER—AUXILIARY RANGE
N STARTING SWITCH
O TEMPERATURE GAGE
P ACCELERATOR FOOT REST
Q SPEEDOMETER
R ACCELERATOR (FOOT THROTTLE)
S OIL PRESSURE GAGE
T FUEL GAGE
U BRAKE PEDAL
V INSTRUMENT PANEL LIGHT SWITCH
W CLUTCH PEDAL
X FUEL TANK
Y FIRE EXTINGUISHER
Z SAFETY STRAP
AA HEADLIGHT FOOT SWITCH (BEAM CONTROL)
AB BLACKOUT LIGHT SWITCH
AC BLACKOUT DRIVING LIGHT SWITCH
AD REAR VISION MIRROR
AE CHOKE CONTROL
AF IGNITION SWITCH
AG HAND THROTTLE
AH RIFLE HOLDER

5. USE OF INSTRUMENTS AND CONTROLS IN VEHICULAR OPERATION

a. Before-operation Service. Perform the services in paragraph 13 before attempting to start the engine.

b. Starting Engine. To start the engine proceed as follows:

(1) Put transmission gearshift lever in neutral position.
(2) Pull out hand throttle button about ¾ inch to 1 inch.
(3) Pull out choke button all the way. NOTE: *Choking is not necessary when engine is warm.*
(4) Turn ignition to "ON" position.
(5) Depress clutch pedal to disengage clutch, and hold pedal down while engine is started.
(6) Step on starting switch to crank again. Release switch as soon as engine starts.
(7) Adjust choke and throttle control buttons to obtain proper idling speed. As engine warms up, push choke button all the way in.
(8) Check oil pressure gage reading; at idle speed the indicator hand should show at least 10 on the gage.
(9) Check ammeter for charge reading. Check fuel gage for indication of fuel supply.
(10) After engine has operated a few minutes, check temperature gage reading. Normal operating temperature is between 160°F and 185°F.
(11) In extremely cold weather refer to paragraph 7.

c. Placing Vehicle in Motion.

(1) For daytime driving turn on service stop light (par. 4 b (2)).
(2) Place transfer case right-hand shift lever in rear position to engage "HIGH" range, then place center shift lever in forward position to disengage front axle.
(3) Depress clutch pedal, and move transmission shift lever toward driver and backward to engage low (1st) gear.
(4) Release parking (hand) brake.
(5) Slightly depress accelerator to increase engine speed, and at the same time slowly release clutch pedal, increasing pressure on accelerator as clutch engages and vehicle starts to move. NOTE: *During the following operations perform procedures outlined in paragraph 14.*
(6) Increase speed to approximately 10 miles per hour, depress clutch pedal, and at the same time release pressure on accelerator. Move transmission shift lever out of low gear into neutral, and then into

second gear. No double clutching is required. Release clutch pedal and accelerate engine.

(7) After vehicle has attained a speed of approximately 20 miles per hour, follow the same procedure as outlined above in order to shift into high (3rd) gear, moving the gearshift lever straight back.

d. Shifting to Lower Gears in Transmission. Shift to a lower gear before engine begins to labor, as follows: Depress clutch pedal quickly, shift to next lower gear, increase engine speed, release clutch pedal slowly, and accelerate. When shifting to a lower gear at any rate of vehicle speed, make sure that the engine speed is synchronized with vehicle speed before clutch is engaged.

e. Shifting Gears in Transfer Case. The transfer case is the means by which power is applied to the front and rear axles. In addition, the low gear provided by the transfer case further increases the number of speeds provided by the transmission. The selection of gear ratios depends upon the road and load conditions. Shift gears in the transfer case in accordance with the shift plate, and observe the instructions on the caution plate. The transmission gearshift does not in any way affect the selection or shifting of the transfer case gears. Vehicle may be driven by rear axle, or by both front and rear axles. The front axle cannot be driven independently.

(1) FRONT AXLE ENGAGEMENT. Front axle should be engaged only in off-the-road operation, slippery roads, steep grades, or during hard pulling. Disengage front axle when operating on average roads under normal conditions.

(a) Engaging Front Axle with Transfer Case in "HIGH" Range. With transfer case in "HIGH" range, move front axle drive shift lever to "IN" position. Depressing the clutch pedal will facilitate shifting.

(b) Disengaging Front Axle with Transfer Case in "HIGH" Range. Move front axle drive shift lever to "OUT" position. Depress the clutch pedal to facilitate shifting.

(c) Disengaging Front Axle when Transfer Case is in "LOW."

1. Depress clutch pedal, then shift transfer case lever into "HIGH."
2. Shift front axle drive lever into "OUT" position.
3. Release clutch pedal and accelerate engine to desired speed.

(2) ENGAGING TRANSFER CASE LOW RANGE. Transfer case LOW range cannot be engaged until front axle drive is engaged.

(a) Engage front axle drive (subpar. e (1) above).

(b) Depress clutch pedal and move transfer case shift lever into "N" (neutral) position.

(c) Release clutch pedal and accelerate engine.

(d) Depress clutch pedal again and move transfer case shift lever forward into "LOW" position.

(e) Release clutch pedal, and accelerate engine to desired speed.

(3) ENGAGING TRANSFER CASE– "LOW" TO "HIGH." This shift can be made regardless of vehicle speed.

(a) Depress clutch pedal and move transfer case shift lever into "HIGH" position.

(b) Release clutch pedal, and accelerate engine to desired speed.

f. Stopping the Vehicle. Remove foot from accelerator, and apply brakes by depressing brake pedal.

(1) When vehicle speed has been reduced to engine idle speed, depress clutch pedal and move transmission shift lever to "N" (neutral) position.

(2) When vehicle has come to a complete stop, apply parking (hand) brake, and release clutch and brake pedals.

g. Reversing the Vehicle. To shift into reverse speed, first bring the vehicle to a complete stop.

(1) Depress clutch pedal.

(2) Move transmission shift lever to the left and forward into "R" (reverse) position.

(3) Release clutch pedal slowly, and accelerate as load is picked up.

h. Stopping the Engine. To stop the engine turn the ignition switch to "OFF" position. NOTE: *Before a new or reconditioned vehicle is first put into service: make run-in tests as outlined in section 10.*

CHAPTER 8

THE BREN LIGHT MACHINE GUN

Description, Use and Mechanism, Undated

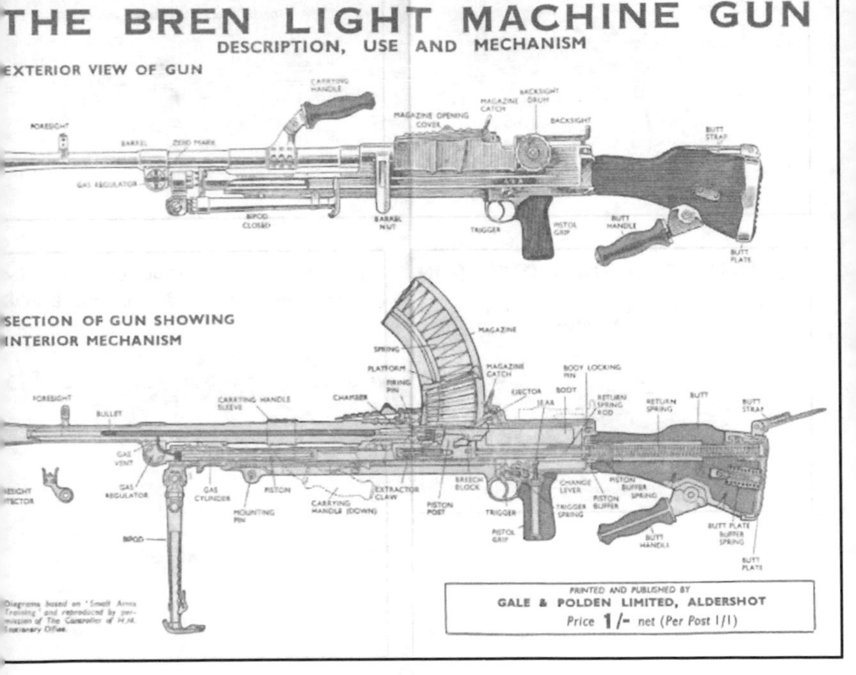

1 THE GUN IS GAS OPERATED

Some of the gas, formed by the explosion of the cartridge, passes through the GAS REGULATOR and operates the piston

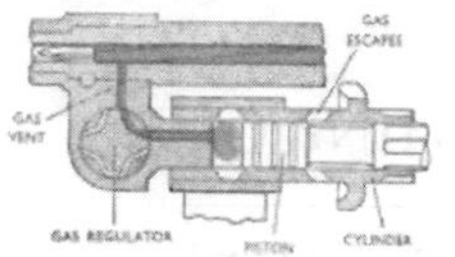

GAS REGULATOR

2 IT IS AIR COOLED

After firing ten magazines at the RAPID rate the barrel should be changed. This operation takes a trained man 6 to 8 seconds.

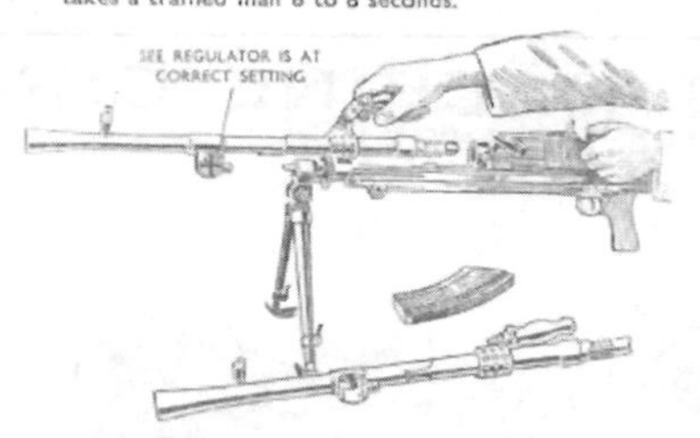

3 IT IS FED BY A MAGAZINE holding 30 Rounds

AMMUNITION is removed from chargers

HOLD THE MAGAZINE AND CHARGER IN ONE HAND

GRIP ROUNDS AND REMOVE FROM CHARGER

The MAGAZINE can be filled by hand in 40 seconds

EACH ROUND PRESSED DOWN WITH THUMB

MAGAZINE RESTED ON THIGH

or by the FILLER in 20 seconds

MAGAZINE

OPERATING LEVER

MAGAZINE CATCH

CHARGER READY FOR LOADING INTO MAGAZINE

TIP OF OPERATING LEVER

4 LOADING is a SIMPLE OPERATION

The front end of the magazine is inserted first and then pressed downwards till the catch engages

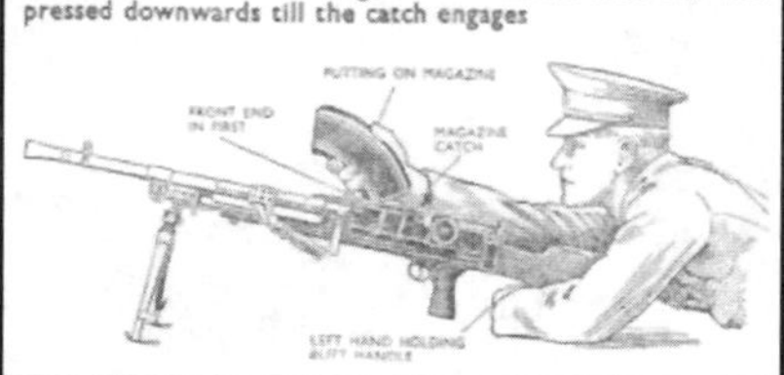

5 THE GUN is shoulder controlled and normally fired from the BIPOD

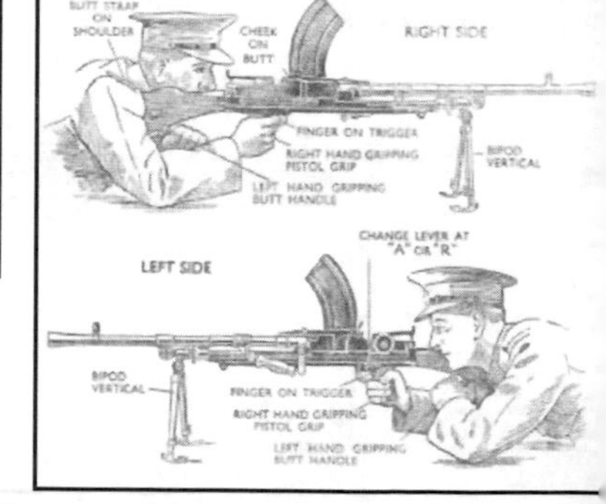

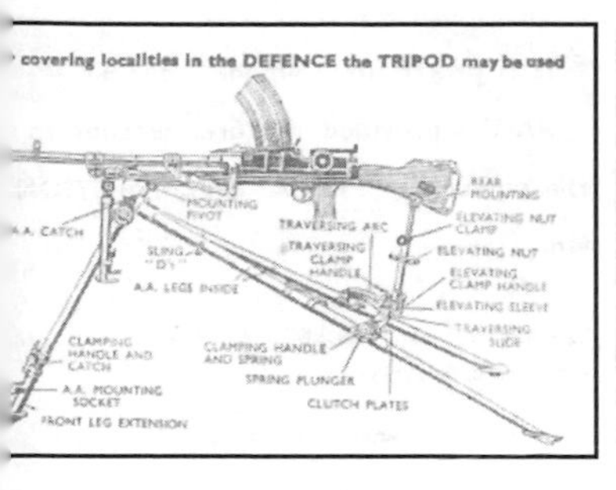

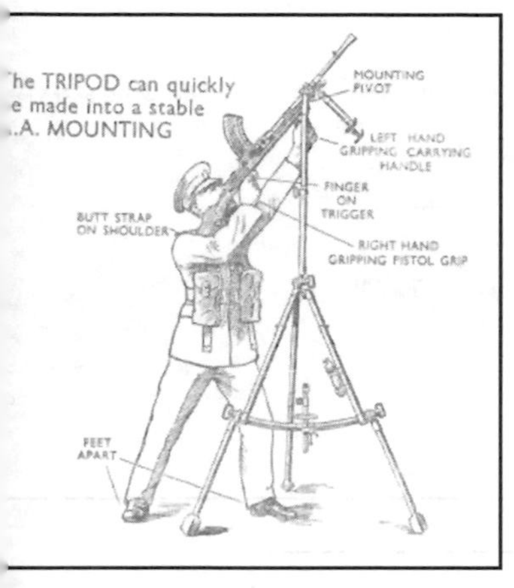

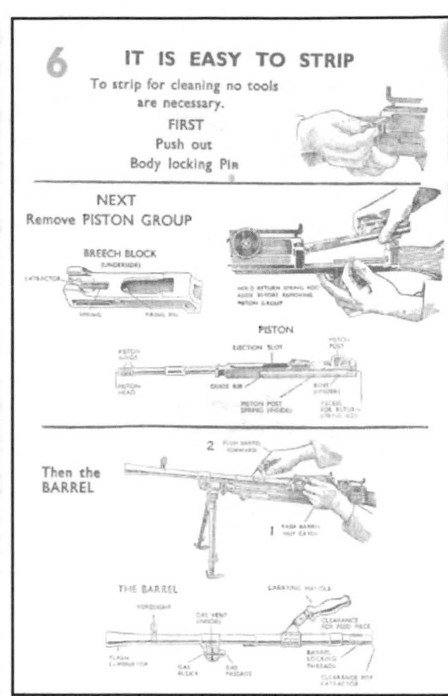

ASSEMBLE IN THE REVERSE ORDER —

IT CANNOT BE ASSEMBLED INCORRECTLY

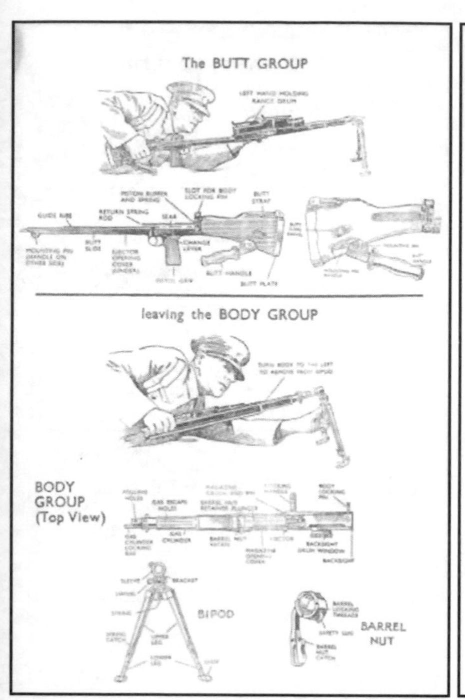

7 **It is practically immune from STOPPAGES provided the firer attends to the points in "PREPARE FOR ACTION which are—**

EXAMINE Foresight, GAS REGULATOR, Bipod, Barrel N Catch and Backsight.

TEST mechanism to ensure free working.

EXAMINE EACH MAGAZINE to see that the top cartridg is correctly positioned.

IMPORTANT—Ensure that cartridges are not rim behind rim

CORRECT

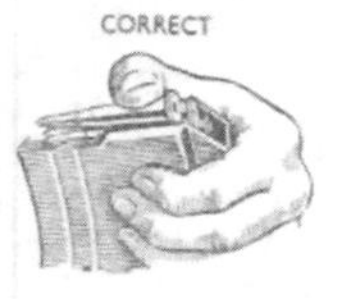

INCORRECT

8 **THERE IS ONLY ONE "IMMEDIATE ACTION"**

If the gun fails to fire or stops firing—

PULL BACK COCKING HANDLE
MAGAZINE OFF
PRESS TRIGGER
MAGAZINE ON*
COCK GUN, AIM AND FIRE

* The magazine which has been removed is examined to see if empty ; if not, that the top rounds are correctly positioned. If the rounds in the magazine are correct and it is reasonably full, the same magazine will be used.

If, after applying I.A., the gun fires one or two rounds and stops again—

Pull back cocking handle and remove magazine, press trigger, cock gun, disconnect the barrel, and adjust the gas regulator to the next largest hole—replace the barrel —place magazine on, aim and fire.

It is capable of firing "BURSTS" or "SINGLE ROUNDS"

by moving the change lever to "A" or "R"

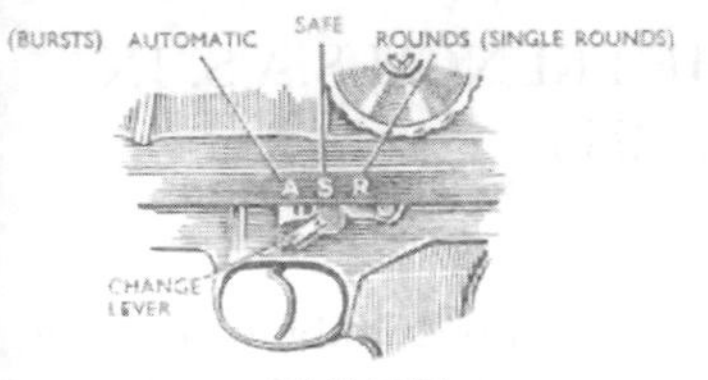

"S" IS SAFE

The NORMAL rate of **AUTOMATIC** is 5 rsts of 4 or 5 rounds, or one MAGAZINE r minute.

SINGLE ROUNDS are used to economise munition and conceal the presence of an JTOMATIC weapon.

APID FIRE (Four MAGAZINES per minute) only for **EMERGENCIES.**

10 THE MECHANISM IS SIMPLE

1. Backward Action. Some of the gases following the **bullet** pass through the **gas vent** and **gas regulator** into the **gas cylinder.** This forces the **piston** to the rear and compresses the **return spring** until the **piston** is stopped by the **piston buffer.** The empty case, being gripped by the **extractor,** is carried to the rear on the face of the **breech block** until its base meets the **ejector.** The case is then ejected downwards through the **ejection slot** in the **piston.**

2. Forward Action. The **piston,** carrying the **breech block,** having been stopped by the **piston buffer** is forced forward by the **return spring.** The **feed piece** meets the base of the first round in the **magazine** and forces it forward into the **chamber,** the **extractor** closing over the rim. The **piston post** in its final move forward drives the **firing pin** against the cap of the cartridge, thus firing the round.

3. Trigger Action. With the **change lever at " Automatic "** pressure on the **trigger** disengages the **sear** from **the bent** on the **piston,** and the **piston** is allowed to go forward. As long as the **trigger** is pressed the gun will continue to fire, but if the **trigger** is released the **bent** will engage with the **sear** the next time the **piston** comes to the rear stopping its forward movement.

With the **change lever** at **" Rounds "** the **trigger** must be pressed each time a shot is to be fired, because the **piston** is held back after each round.

With the change lever at **" Safe "** the **trigger** is disengaged from the **sear,** and the gun cannot be fired.

If pressure on the **trigger** is maintained while the **change lever** is altered from **" Safe "** to **" Automatic "** and then released and **trigger** pressed again, gun will not fire. The **change lever,** therefore, will not be altered while the **trigger** is pressed.

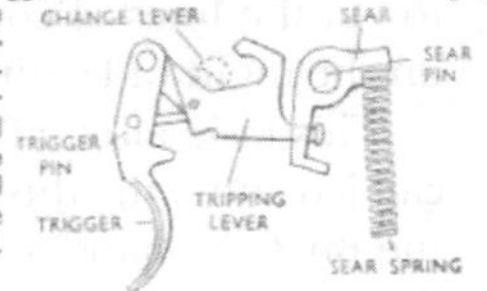

11

ELEVATION is obtained by turning the RANGE DRUM

500x

EMEMBER! IT IS LIGHT, MOBILE AND RIMARILY A "ONE MAN WEAPON"

CHAPTER 9

LOOKING BACK TO THE FRENCH S.A.S. IN BRITTANY, 1944

This true narrative of the exploits of the S.A.S has been submitted by the officer who took part in them. All names have been changed for obvious reasons.
The Editor

INTRODUCTION

The Allied Invasion Plan of 1944 included the dropping of S.A.S. parties to cut the lines of communication joining Brittany to the rest of France on the night of D minus 1.

This task, allotted to the 2nd [sic] French S.A.S. Bn. was successfully carried out with the assistance of the local Maquis. On its completion the Bn. Commander, Colonel Blanc [Bourgoin], was ordered to organise the speedy arming and training of the Breton Maquis with a view to their playing their part in subsequent operations by the Allied Army in Brittany.

In the South the Bn. Commander met with such enthusiasm from the local inhabitants that he proceeded to call up the Maquis, and by 13 June had formed a camp of 6,000 men at St. Marcel (Morbihan) to whom no less than thirty aeroplanes had dropped arms in one night. This camp of untrained men was subsequently attacked by the Germans on the 18th June. A battle raged all day, and during the night the S.A.S. and Maquis disappeared into thin air, having killed some 400–500 Germans and only losing a combined total of approximately 30.

The last signal received in England from the Colonel was to the effect that his camp was surrounded and that he could not continue to keep the wireless open in case the Germans pin-pointed his exact location with their detector apparatus.

Meanwhile smaller and equally premature concentrations of the Maquis and S.A.S. in other parts of Brittany had been attacked and dispersed, with the result that the Bde. Commander at his Headquarters

in London had some 300–400 men launched in Brittany and was out of contact with them all. No signals were received from anyone for three days – on the third day the Brigadier decided to send me to the South to re-establish contact. I took with me a fresh radio team of three Frenchman, my own English batman, another French Officer and two French parachutists. We went the same night – there was no moon nor was there anyone on the ground to signal the location of a reconnoitred dropping zone to the pilot. The pilot and I selected a likely spot off the map, and he did his best, with the aid of "George" to put us out over it. In actual fact we arrived about seven miles wide of the mark, but we all landed safely in the right general area at about 3 a.m.

GAINING CONTACT

The fact that we were being dropped on that particular night had been broadcast in code over the B.B.C. and we had been allotted a code sentence to be broadcast on the European Services at special times for the next two days to help us establish our authenticity with any well-disposed locals. Apart from hiding our parachutes and kitbags, we did nothing until dawn except move a few kilometres away from where we actually landed. Being combatant troops we were, of course, all in ordinary parachutist uniform.

Our efforts the next day to make contact with the local farmers were not very successful – although they were not hostile they disclaimed all knowledge of the Maquis or any battle or of the one-armed Colonel Blanc [Bourgoin]. This was hardly surprisingly as the Germans had captured many of our uniforms, and, dressed in them, were doing exactly as I was in order to chase down the S.A.S. who were lying up in the area.

During the day the party split in two and moved off by different routes to a rendezvous in the woods where I had decided we should stay the night. We missed each other that night and did not meet again until the following morning, the other half having also failed to make useful contacts. We moved on again, and, at about midday, having chosen a safe lying-up place for the rest of the party, I moved off with one Frenchman to tackle various farmers. After talking to one or two who were unresponsive I came across one who, while denying all knowledge of everything connected with the Maquis, gave me the impression that he would have helped had he been confident of our authenticity. He explained that if, after he had given us information about the Maquis, we turned out to be Germans, his wife and five children would probably be shot and his farm

burnt. It was unfortunate at this stage that the Frenchman accompanying me was an Alsacien who spoke French with a German accent!

We left the farmer saying we would come back at 6 p.m. with our wireless and he could listen to our phrase which I told him would be broadcast at 6. (This, incidentally, was the last broadcast.) We duly came back, tuned in to the Service, but by the time it was all set we were too late for the broadcast. However, the farmer was a good chap and was sufficiently impressed with our English equipment and our wireless set to have some confidence in us. He agreed to take my identity card and that of the French Officer accompanying me which he would show to some of his friends whom he thought knew the whereabouts of some of the S.A.S. These latter, if they recognized us from photographs, might be able to put us in touch with the Colonel. As a result of this, two days later a guide collected me in the morning and took me to a cottage where the Colonel had his Headquarters. At this time the whole area was full of Germans hunting for him and they had put a large price on his head, but in spite of this he had re-opened his wireless communications with Bde. Headquarters. We, therefore decided, in order to avoid having two wirelesses operating in the same place and also to avoid swelling the numbers of his Headquarters, that I should go with my party to join Captain Maurice near Tredion. This Officer was one of the S.A.S. Company Commanders who was controlling the Maquis in that particular area. This part of Brittany consists of very small fields surrounded by high banks and hedges and has few main roads but hundreds of winding lanes. For this reason we were able to dodge the Germans and go from one place to another, even by day, provided we had a good guide.

ARMING THE MAQUIS

Our task was to arm and train as many Maquis as possible but not to concentrate them in large numbers until ordered to do so from London. We were told that, in all probability, a subsidiary landing would take place somewhere in Brittany during the coming full-moon period.

The general system which was adopted by all Commanders in the area for arming and training the Maquis was now roughly the same. This was to farm out their trained soldiers to each group of Maquis, and then the Commander, through his wireless link with London, would arrange for each group to be supplied with arms and equipment in turn in their own area. The system worked well as no large concentration of Maquisards was necessary for a drop of arms to any one place, and also the local

Commander kept control of each group as it depended on him for its arms, ammunition and also money.

Capt Maurice's headquarters was between 16 and 20 strong and was situated around the edges of a field with sentries posted at each corner. In spite of the incessant rain they did not go into the farm even at night and all their food was provided by the neighbouring farmers. I stayed with Maurice for a few days and assisted in the re-organization of the various Maquis Bns. in this area. For our communications to London and to the other H.Q. groups in Brittany we used wireless. As each group was on a different net to London, direct communication between groups was not possible, but London could relay messages as requested. Our communication on the ground was by means of runners called locally "agents de liaison". The majority of these were young girls between the ages of sixteen and twenty-five who at this stage were not suspected by the Germans and who were allowed to circulate freely. Even if stopped they were seldom searched. Later on some were captured and tortured by the Germans for information, but none gave anything away.

After I had been with Maurice about a week I was ordered by Brigade Headquarters to go northwards to join Captain David and his group near Guern, a distance of about 40 kilometres as the crow flies and considerably more by the devious route we were forced to take. The area was still full of German detachments who actually were Russians with German officers, a proportion of them being mounted and known locally as Cossacks. We, therefore, made most of the journey at night or in the middle of the day (when the Germans were eating) on foot through the lanes. I took with me my wireless team and my batman. The French Officer and two men were left with Captain Maurice.

Within 48 hours of my leaving Maurice's Headquarters it was surprised at night and all in it, with the exception of two, were taken prisoner and subsequently shot or, as in the case of Maurice himself, tortured to death. The reason for this disaster was that French miliciens working for the Gestapo had infiltrated into the camp at night dressed as parachutists. In my opinion Maurice stayed too long in the same place and his presence there was much too widely known in the area. At the best of times the French are not security-minded – when one is dealing with enthusiastic peasants with a liking for strong cider, it is impossible to keep anything secret.

Our trip to Guern was uneventful except for one rather tricky period when we crossed the river Blavet at about midday. We were paddling over

in a very unseaworthy little rowing boat, and one of the oars which were rotten broke in two and we were left in the middle of the river with the boat going rapidly downstream in circles. However, eventually we got across without being noticed. We also visited on the way up about four small Maquis and arranged for arms to be dropped to them.

It was my experience that the best way to go from one place to another, even if one knew the exact location of one's destination, was to be handed on from guide to guide, and never to take any one guide for any great distance. The inhabitants of this part of Brittany were very primitive and, although knowing their immediate surroundings like the back of their hands, had no idea of the lanes outside a radius of about five miles from their own farms.

Captain David had his Headquarters organized differently from Maurice's. It consisted only of himself, his wireless team of three, one parachutist, and his "agent de liaison". He only stayed in one place for about forty-eight hours, and only a few people with whom he was 100 per cent. sure knew his exact location. During the day he kept well away from buildings but at night he went into the lofts of farms. He successfully arranged almost nightly parachutings of arms and equipment to all the various Maquis in his sector over which he had an extraordinary high measure of control.

Meanwhile, the weather continued to be so bad that the moon period came and went without any subsidiary landing being possible. This meant that the parachutists and the Maquis would have to wait either for the next full-moon or until the breakthrough in Normandy took place before being relieved. Every day more and more of the Maquis leaders and the S.A.S. were being rounded up, and this fact, not unnaturally, was beginning to affect the morale of those who were left.

After I had been with David about a week and the battle at Caen was in full swing, I received a signal ordering me to return to England as soon as possible and to contact a man named Robert at a certain spot in the north of Brittany referred to in the signal simply by a map reference – actually in the vicinity of Guingamp. This Robert was to put me into the M.I.9 escape channel. As Guingamp was some 70 kilometres away, I decided to make the journey in a car at night. Before leaving David I had been given maps showing some details of the defence plans of the ports of Morlaix in the north and Vannes and Lorient in the south. These I was to take with me to England. I left my wireless team with David and set off with only my batman and the two Maquisard owners of the car. The driver left us on the road near to where Robert was supposed to be and went home. At first light we approached the farm and the farmer denied all knowledge of anyone of the name of Robert. We then went to the outskirts of the nearest village and asked another man if he had heard of Robert. No such man existed and nor was there anyone in the village except one very old yokel who even had the Christian name of Robert.

So there I was with all contacts broken and in a hell of a hurry to get to London with my maps and other information!

I regretted very much having broken my principle of always being handed on from contact to contact. It was obvious that I had received a corrupted map reference from the Brigade Headquarters but as I had left my wireless sending sat behind at Guern I had no way of getting a correction. I was obviously going to waste all the time I had saved by my car journey before I could get in touch with Robert.

REGAINING CONTACT

After going up to several people we eventually found one youngish man who seemed helpful. I put our position to him and did my best to convince him of our bona fides. I arranged with him that we should go and lie up in a small wood well away from the lanes and that he should come back to us at midday with some food, and that in the meantime he should report our presence to the head of the local Maquis. From his point of view, this was a sound arrangement, but from ours it was not quite so good because, had he gone to the Germans instead of to the Maquis, we should not have known until it was too late. He came back as arranged, not only with food, but also with an active Maquisard called "Tristan" who said that he had heard of Robert, would tell him that we were in the area, and that if Robert had information about us from London he would send guides to fetch us the following day.

I explained to "Tristan" that we were in a hurry and that Robert was going to arrange for our swift return to England. He then told us that he knew of an R.A.F. Serjeant-Pilot who had been shot down and was hiding in the area, but who had not been able to find anybody to help him to get home. I decided that he should join us the following day and go with us to Robert. We spent that night in the farm we had visited that morning where the old man, now reassured that we were British, was only too pleased to have us.

ROBERT'S MAQUIS

The next morning the Serjeant-Pilot joined us, and in the afternoon the three of us set off with Robert's guides to join his Maquis some miles away. This Maquis was by far the most efficient I had seen. Although Robert was only a young Serjeant in the French S.A.S. Battalion, it was he that commanded this Maquis consisting of some two hundred men – all the officers (mostly French Army Reserve officers) willingly accepted him as their Commanding Officer. The camp itself was in a large wood near a big lake, and the inmates really conducted themselves as trained soldiers. Guards were mounted properly, organized parades held, and the Tricolour was hoisted with due ceremony at dawn and similarly lowered at dusk. Strong pickets guarded every approach to the wood and Robert had even put anti-personnel mines round what he considered the most dangerous approaches. These mines stood him in good stead when his camp was attacked by the Germans shortly after I had left him.

While at Robert's camp, where we stayed two days, we were joined by another British S.A.S. liaison officer, Sqn.-Ldr. Pat Smith, and also by an American Army Air Force Major, who, like the Serjeant-Pilot, had been shot down some weeks before. Our party for the homeward journey was, therefore, five.

We had to stay at Robert's camp for two days (a) to turn ourselves into civilians, and (b) so as to give time for the M.I.9 contacts to arrange for us to be collected by the Royal Navy from the coast. We all had passport photographs taken, and false identity cards were prepared for us by the local Mayor. My batman was yokel, and I was a shipping agent. We were dressed in plain clothes accordingly, but contrary to the normal practice on these occasions, we all kept arms and grenades. It seemed strange to us not to be in uniform and theoretically to be able to go where we liked.

M.I.9 CHANNELS

In the early morning of the third day of our stay with Robert we left in a farm cart driven by one of the Maquis for our first staging post on our route to the coast. We had about thirty kilometres to go, and as usual our destination was a small unobtrusive little farm. On the way, feeling somewhat overconfident of our disguise, I suggested to our driver that we should stop at a bistro and have a drink. To this he agreed with alacrity, and we went into a small cafe. I ordered a Calvados to which, unfortunately, my companions were unused, and, not realising how strong it was, swallowed a good gulp each. The splutterings which followed not unnaturally attracted the attention of the other people in the cafe, so as soon as my companions had recovered sufficiently we left in haste!

The rest of our trip was uneventful. At the farm we met the head of the M.I.9 organization for that particular part of the world – a Canadian called Lt. "Labrosse" who had been doing this job for just under a year. He told us that his orders were to get me home as soon as possible, but so far he has not been able to make the final arrangements for a boat. He did not stay long with us and said that he would be back in the evening.

That evening he came to our farm and took me off to his hide-out. There he explained to me that normally we should have waited for two days at the farm, but as it was so urgent he had managed to arrange for our getaway the following night. This meant that later on in the early part of the night we should have to move on foot to our last "staging" farm. He also told me that I was the first person he had ever actually shown where he lived – it was in a loft! Normally, he always arranges to meet all his agents and contacts at cafes or anywhere other than where he had his wireless link to England. His radio operator was also a Canadian, and one of the toughest men I have ever seen.

I rejoined the others, and we waited for nightfall to be guided to the last farm.

Apart from having to cross roads on which the Germans had motorized patrols – we were very near the coast by this time – the journey was quite simple.

THE LAST HALT

We arrived at the farm and all was in darkness. "Labrosse" said that in our case he had not had time to warn the farmer that we were coming. However, he was soon woken up and lit a lamp, and we went in. Then, thirsty and hungry after the long walk, we had some cider and chocolate and biscuits before being dispersed to the various lofts to sleep.

Our Canadian friend left us, and we had been chatting for about a quarter of an hour when suddenly there were shouts outside and a few rounds from a rifle were fired through the door. Obviously a patrol had come on the farm and, as we found out later, the farmer, who had not been expecting us, had not put up his black-out. Pat Smith had the presence of mind to dash out the light and the farmer just had time to push us up some stairs into the loft before unlocking his door.

Luckily one of us had a torch and at once we saw that the loft was divided into two by a wall with a doorway in it. We stumbled into the far compartment while downstairs the farmer's wife wailed and screamed to

try to drown the noise of our steps. She had a baby of two months old who helped to swell the racket!

The patrol, all Russians, had seen through the window that there were obviously more people in the house than just the farmer and his wife, and finding some of our English sweets and biscuits on the table downstairs, shouted up the stairs demanding that we should come down.

Upstairs we were in a tricky position; in plain clothes, all armed and I with the ports defence plans on me. Furthermore, I knew the location of the Canadian's hideout. If we came down, we were obviously going to have a very bad time – we all knew the fate of so many of our friends. There was no way out of the loft except by the stairs. (Usually in these lofts there was a sort of window by which the corn could be loaded, and by which people like ourselves could escape). If we tried to blast our way out by throwing a couple of grenades down the stairs we would have blown the farmer and his wife to bits as well as the patrol.

The only hope seemed to be to stay where we were behind the wall dividing the loft, and if they came up after us to lob the grenades into the other half and hope that the thin wall between us would protect us. Of course, it was far more likely that they would sit tight, send for reinforcements, surround the building, and then burn it down – quite a normal practice.

We waited and meanwhile downstairs the shouts for us or even two of us to go down increased, and the screams of the woman got more and more voluble. Suddenly another shot was fired, there was a shout of pain and piercing screams from the woman. Our visions of what might be going on downstairs were appalling but we made no move and the demands for us to go down ceased. Instead, thick voices demanded "cognac", and, to our relief, we heard the farmer answer that he had some, and he produced it.

Shortly afterwards someone went out and again a little later on we heard a cart arrive. Naturally, in our frame of mind, we imagined reinforcements, but we stayed still and listened. To our amazement we heard a lot of shuffling downstairs, some comparatively subdued talk, everyone going outside, the cart moving off, and then, for a few moments – silence. A minute later we heard running feet in the parlour and on the stairs and the farmer was with us. He said that the Russians had gone and it was the one chance for us to get to hell out of it. He did not have to tell us twice. In a moment we had gone, but the second before we dashed off, I managed to arrange with him roughly where we would be – lying under a hedge about three fields away in the direction he pointed.

THE LAST LAP

Just at first light, we heard footsteps coming in our direction. We peered through the top of the corn in the half light of the morning, and to our relief, we saw Labrosse and our farmer. We were at once taken off on foot to a safer hiding place in a thicket some five or six miles away. On the way we sometimes redoubled on our tracks to confuse any German police dogs which might be tracking us. We thought of dogs for the whole of the rest of that day!

Apparently, what had happened in the farm was that the farmer had been standing on the first of the stairs that led up to our loft with two Russians below covering him from either side of the entrance to the staircase. Luckily they were slightly drunk, and when he made a move to pass them and go down into the parlour, one of them loosed off his trigger, but, instead of getting the farmer, he hit his fellow-countryman opposite. From that moment the whole patrol temporarily lost interest in us and concentrated on the badly-wounded man. The farmer at once suggested that his friend from next door had a horse and cart in which the Russian could be taken back to the camp, and so it was that they all left and we were able to slip away. They did not forget about us or the farm for long because at dawn they came and burned it to the ground. By that time the farmer had hidden his wife and child in a friend's farm nearby and arrangements were made for him to join our party for England.

All the next day we lay up in the thicket and that night we were guided down to the beach. A young girl led us through the minefield – she put white handkerchiefs or rags on each mine along the path, and we followed in single file after her, being very careful not to step on the white patches.

We were picked up according to plan, the Navy arriving within literally a few seconds of the time arranged. By midday we were at Brigade Headquarters, and that night, having made my report and arranged the conferences for the morrow, I went in a party to the Dorchester, and I don't think Bollinger '28 has ever tasted so good!

CHAPTER 10

OPERATIONS OF THE 4TH FRENCH PARABATTALION

This account of the 4th Bn's operations is compiled from the information available up to the 30th June, 1944.

The 4th Bn's task included:

(a) The severance of communications between Britanny [sic] and the rest of France in order to prevent reinforcements located in the province from coming to the assistance of enemy troops engaged in the beach-head area.

(b) The recruiting, arming and organizing of resistance elements in Britanny, in conjunction with representatives of SFHQ.

As far as could be ascertained before D Day, enemy troops in Britanny included:—

1 Div. at RENNES (possibly the 17 SS Pz Gr)
The 721 Inf. Div. at DINAN.
Elements of the 5th Para Div. West of RENNES
The 25 Inf Div. at VANNES.
The 265 Inf Div. at LORIENT.
The 3rd Para Div. in the area of CARHAIX.
The 353 Div at MORLAIX.
The 343 Inf Div. NW of BREST
The 266 Inf Div. in the ST BRIEUC – GUINGAMP Area

On the other hand, although it was known that the Province of BRITANNY was one of those most strongly imbued with the spirit of resistance, it was not, for a number of reasons, anticipated that the 4th Bn would come into contact, on landing, with any readily organised force and be in a position to start operations at a moment's notice.

Task (a) was entrusted to a number of parties, 18 altogether, who were dropped in the night of D + 1/D + 2 (7 to 8 June).

Their main task was to cut railway communications, and, if possible, make a job of it by bringing about the derailment of a train. After having achieved this, they were to carry out more attacks on railway lines, sever telecommunications and deal with targets of opportunity. Lastly they would make their way back to one of the established bases (see further).

Hereunder are names of party leaders, numbers in each party, and the main task assigned to it. The exact location of the cuts had been set out as well as the DZs, but on being briefed, most of the party leaders chose to alter these, and there is no available record of their final choice. The tasks are therefore given without map references.

Party Leader	**No. of Men**	**Task**	
Lt VIAUD	3	cut railway between	ST.BRIEUC – GUINGAMP
Sgt ROQUEMAURE	3	" " "	LAMBALLE – CAULNES
Aspt FAUQUET	3	" " "	LAMBALLE – DANAN
S/Lt APRIOU	3	" " "	LA BROHINIERE – DINAN
Sgt CARRE	3	" " "	LA BROHINIERE – REMMES
S/Lt VARNIER	5	" " "	MESSAC – RENNES
S/Lt DE CAMARET	5	" " "	MESSAC – REDON
Lt TISNE	3	" " "	REDON – CHATEAUBRIANT
S/Ch NICOL	3	" " "	REDON – PONT CHATEAU
Lt MAIRET	3	" " "	REDON – QUESTEMBERT
S/Lt SKINNER	3	" " "	QUESTEMBERT – VANNES
S/Lt BRES	3	" " "	PLOERMEL – MESSAC
Sgt MENDES CALDAS	3	" " "	PLOERMEN [sic] – QUESTEMBERT
Capt LARRALDE	3	" " "	AUREY – PONTIVY
S/Lt CORTA	3	" " "	PLOERMEL – ST. MEEN
S/Lt LEGRAND	3	" " "	ST. MEEN – LOUDEAC
S/Lt FERNANDEZ	3	" " "	LOUDEAC – ST. BRIEUC
Capt DE MAUDUIT	3	" " "	LOUDEAC – CARHAIX

The parties took off from BRIZE–NORTON in 9 Albemarles, each aircraft taking two sticks.

Very little news has come in so far on the success of these parties. It is only known that Captain LARRALDE, Lt. MAIRET, S/Lt SKINNER and Sgt MENDES CALDAS have joined the DINGSON base, after completing their respective tasks.

It also appears from the report of a pilot, and messages received by carrier pigeon, that on some occasions ruck-sacs were lost in the drop, and on others, exploded on reaching the ground.

A further report suggested that several of the tasks had already been performed by partisans when the operational parties arrived. At all events, the disruption caused in the enemy's communications was satisfactorily thorough. Further operational parties from base areas contributed to keep up this state of havoc, and railway communications can be said to have been almost permanently interrupted between BRITANNY and the rest of FRANCE since soon after the invasion started.

The first step in the carrying out of task (b) was the establishment of two bases, one in the LANDES DES LANVAUX, in the neighbourhood of MALESTROIT (between VANNES and PLOERMEL), under the code name of DINGSON; the other east of CALLAC and SW of GUINGAMP (W 7595, W 9295, W 7582) called SAMWEST.

This was effected by two parties of 18 under Lt MARIENNE (DINGSON) with Lt DEPLANTE as 2nd i/c and Lt DESCHAMPS (SAMWEST) with Lt BOTELLA as 2nd i/c.

In order to make doubly sure, the parties were split up into two sticks of 9 and emplaned in two different aircraft (Stirlings), so that half of one party was to be dropped from the same aircraft as half of the other, each aircraft being flown over both bases. It was thus hoped to ensure the safe arrival in each base of at least 1 officer and 8 ORs with two WT sets.

Lt HUBERT of Special Forces was also dropped with Lt MARIENNE's stick.

The parties took off from FAIRFORD AERODROME after 2300 hrs on 5th June.

The arrangements described above proved most useful in the case of DINGSON.

Lt MARIENNE was dropped by mistake over a German camp. His three radio operators and another man were captured or killed. Lt. MARIENNE and the four others managed to escape and joined Lt DEPLANTE on the 8th.

Meanwhile, Lt DEPLANTE had been in a position to start work at the newly established base, and it was reported on the 8th that contact had been made with an organization numbering 3500 men who were, however, still unarmed.

Further contacts were established on the 9th with a White Russian battalion in the RUIS peninsula, who expressed willingness to join our side at H hour. What exactly was meant by this is not yet clear; the Russians do not seem to have been active so far and it is to be feared that, to their way of thinking, H hour really means not the first, but the last hour of operations.

On the other hand, the local gendarmerie seems to have joined our forces almost immediately.

On the following days, the DINGSON party proceeded to build up their strength. A large DZ, 418233, on a plateau west of MALESTROIT, and adjoining a wooded area to the west, was used night after night, weather permitting, strongly guarded on each occasion by several hundreds of partisans.

Reinforcements up to a number of 50 under Captain PUECH-SAMSON, were dropped on the night of the 9th and Comdt BOURGOIN followed with another party of 50 on the 10th. However, on this particular occasion the weather closed down very abruptly over the DZ and only one 'plane carrying the CO was able to drop its load. The other two returned to FAIRFORD with 30 odd men. These were dropped on the 12th together with a third reinforcement of 50 under Lt. GUILLON. Capt FAY accompanied this lot.

A final reinforcement of 40, under Aspt MARIANI, was dropped on the 17th. Altogether, over 200 all ranks were dropped to the DINGSON base.

However, the repeated dropping operations in the same area, the brilliantly lit up DZ and the strong concentration of partisans in the neighbourhood of the base, were bound to attract the enemy's attention. On the 12th, Comdt BOURGOIN signalled that his position was precarious.

On the 14th, he asked for the destruction by bombing of an enemy O.P. on hill 166 (ref H 273267) at a distance of about 10 miles from his base. (This bombing was carried out successfully a few days later). He also asked for the dispatch of machine guns, six pounders and jeeps. Four jeeps was sent on the night of the 17th under S/Lt De la GRANDIERE with a party of 11.

The cars and personnel were dropped successfully, but the containers parachutes with the vickers and ammunitions were Roman candles. This was particularly unfortunate, for Comdt BOURGOIN was attacked next day on the 18th by strong forces in three successive waves: first the field gendarmerie then some Geogien and anti-paratroop forces, and lastly a motorised column with the light armour and artillery.

A mosquito force was detailed to deal with their column but unfortunately arrived too late.

By the end of the day, the enemy had lost 560 killed. The 4th Bn and the partisans, between them, had lost in killed and missing, 250 men. Moreover, they were short of ammunition and unable to withstand a further attack if it had materialised.

Consequently, they dispersed under cover of darkness, taking with them their wounded amongst whom were Capt PUECH-SAMSON and Capt LARRALDE, and part of their stores.

Comdt BOURGOIN's WT was then silent for five days. Later message received from him suggest that this may be due to the danger afforded by enemy detecting apparatus.

A party under Major CARY-ELWES and including Lt. FLEURIOT and 3 WT operators of the 4th Bn was dispatched on the 22nd in order to make contact with Comdt BOURGOIN. It succeeded in this on the 25th.

Comdt BOURGOIN was found in a small hamlet 10 km NW former DZ of MALESTROIT. He was able to report on the position of the men in the former DINGSON Base. These appeared to be dispersed whilst Lt. MARIENNE managed to keep in touch with most of them.

The story of the SAMWEST Base is a very different one.

The advanced base party was dropped successfully under Lt. DESCHAMPS near the forest of DUAULT and south of CALLAC.

Its position was uneasy from the very start and did not foreshadow the great development it was soon to undergo.

The enemy's presence at CALLAC and MAIL–CARHAIX was reported as early as the 7th June and enemy patrols were active at night in the area.

On the other hand, the presence of about 2000 partisans was very encouraging and it was decided to send a reinforcement of 50 under Capt LEBLOND on the night of the 9th. The Bn M.O. was included in the party. This was dropped on DZ 742878, 3 km SW of the Forest of DUAULT.

A further reinforcement was dropped on the 10th including Sq/ Leader SMITH.

It had been hoped to drop a jeep with a team of four on the same night, but the aircraft which was to drop it failed to find the DZ owing to unfavourable weather conditions and returned with its load. Later, Capt LEBLOND indicated that he had not yet any use for jeeps.

The situation was unsettled owing to enemy activities. It was first decided, on the 11th, to shift the DZ to 768893 (on the eastern border of the Forest of DUAULT and on higher ground, thus putting the forest between the DZ and the main enemy local base of CALLAC).

But it was soon found necessary to take more dramatic steps and the whole party proceeded to fall back on the DINGSON base on the 12th.

They were attacked, apparently on the 13th, by a force of 2000 of the enemy and dispersed.

Comdt BOURGOIN then sent Lt DEPLANTE from the DINGSON base to meet the SAMWEST people half way and reorganize them in a new base which was henceforth known as GROG.

On the 16th Lt DEPLANTE reported that he had established a rendezvous for SAMWEST people at 785540, 12 km east of LE FAOUET and about 40 km due south of the former SAMWEST base. 12 men of the SAMWEST party joined the new base on the following day.

Meanwhile, Lt. DEPLANTE had come into contact with two battalions of partisans, one of FTP (Franc-Tireurs et Partisans), and one of FFI (Forces Francaises de l'interieur) for whom bases were selected at MALVOISIN and near LA CROISTY, also in the area 12 km west of LE FAOUET.

The arming and equipping of these forces in the area of GOURIN, LE FAOUET and GUEMENE, proceeded up to the 24th June.

At the same time, another force, an FTP Bn, received equipment at 735622 (3 Km SW of Plouray in the area SW of Rostrenen).

All this work was attended by considerable difficulties, long distances had to be covered for a large number of DZs were used.

Enemy intervention was always to be feared and sometimes actually materialized, as on the 17th when some of our transport was ambushed by the enemy and had to be rescued by a party of patriots; the enemy lost 4 killed and the patriots 2. In the night of 23/24 some of the supplies were dropped near the Germans. There followed what one of the signals called an "animated distribution" of arms and ammunition. One can only guess at what the term implies but on the 24th the GROG commander reported that he was moving to W 950382, 18 K SW of PONTIVY, on the banks of the Blavet.

On the same day, Sq/Leader SMITH also reported that the LE FAOUET–GUEMENE area was by then sufficiently armed and that supply operations were now shifted to the area south of PONTIVY and extended as far east as JOSSELIN. (DZs 060455 and 270415).

By the 27th of June 6 Bns had been formed and were undergoing instruction under the guidance of 70 members of the 4th Bn; it was hoped that three of these would be ready by the end of the week.

The general location of these forces was the western half of the MORBIHAN department. Lt DEPLANTE made it known that he was contemplating the organisation of 5 more Bns in the COTES DU NORD and Sq/Ldr SMITH left for that area accompanied by a number of resistance chiefs.

The prospects of increased action in BRITANNY are further widened by the news that 10,000 men are available in the FINISTERRE for arming and organising.

CHAPTER 11

SUMMARY OF CASUALTIES INFLICTED ON THE ENEMY BY S.A.S. TROOPS DURING OPERATIONS IN 1944

The following figures are compiled from the official reports on operations and only figures definitely quoted have been included. In many instances reports refer to "many enemy killed", "a number of prisoners taken", etc., and no attempt has been made to adjust the figures in this connection.

The results are also exclusive of the damage inflicted on the enemy by the Allied Air Forces as a result of information passed by SAS. 38 different targets are known to have been attacked out of a total of 277 submitted.

Results of Operation "SPENSER" have not yet come to hand.[1]

PERSONNEL

Killed or wounded	7753
PW	4764 (exclusive of 18,000 who surrendered at ISSOUDUN and whose surrender is claimed by 3 French Para Bn to be due to their harassing activities in conjunction with the maquis).

TRANSPORT

Captured	25 lorries
	15 cars
	2 m/c combinations

NOTE [1]. The figures cited here (for enemy personnel killed/wounded/captured) match those in the May 1945 memorandum written by Lieutenant Colonel Collins, extracts from which form Chapter 12, where his note 90. relates to the effect of casualties suffered. Elsewhere, his report cites the human cost to the SAS was "approximately 330 casualties (approximately 16½ per cent)" based upon a force of 2,000 men.

1 bicycle	
Destroyed	348 lorries
	141 cars
	14 AFVs
	57 Horse-drawn vehs
	11 m/c combinations
	13 bicycles
	39 miscellaneous cars

RAILWAYS

Lines out	164
Signal box destroyed	1
trains destroyed	7
trucks destroyed	89
locomotives destroyed	29
derailments	33

BRIDGES

Blown	17

COMMUNICATIONS

Power lines cut	6
Telephone lines and cables	42
Tele: exchanges destd.	3
Roads blocked	10
Aqueducts destroyed	1

MILITARY INSTALLATIONS DESTROYED

Ammunition dumps	7
POL dumps	3 (one containing 100,000 galls)

EQUIPMENT CAPTURED

Ammunition various	600 tons
POL	36,500 litres
Small arms captured	588

MISCELLANEOUS DESTRUCTIONS

Aircraft	1 He. 111 destroyed
	one aircraft probably destroyed

One oil refinery mortared twice
One goods yard destroyed
One gasogene factory destroyed
4 water pumping stations
2 electric power pylons
1 AA Bty
1 Searchlight
2 x 88 mm Mortars
1 x 88 mm gun
1 hy gun
1 x 36 mm mobile gun

MISCELLANEOUS CAPTURES

20 tons wheat

SAS CASUALTIES

The number of SAS troops employed on all operations totals 2252 (no adjustment has been made to this figure in respect of personnel who took part in <u>more than one</u> operation).

Casualties were	Killed or missing or PW	345
	Wounded	115
	(excluding cas of 4 Frn Para Bn in BRITTANY).	

CHAPTER 12

NOTES ON THE ORGANISATION, HISTORY AND EMPLOYMENT OF SPECIAL AIR SERVICE TROOPS

By Lt. Col. Ian G Collins, General Staff Officer, 1 (SAS), 1 Airborne British Corps, May 1945

PART I

INTRODUCTION

1. This pamphlet is intended to give some direction on the organisation and operational role of SAS Troops.

It is unlikely under modern warfare conditions that there will often be, except for short temporary periods, a static defined front line as in the 1914–18 war. The development of air power, with the increased mobility it will give to corps and armies, will tend to make battle areas more fluid.

Two things stand out clearly from the experience gained in operating SAS Troops in this war:

(a) That the dividends paid by introducing small parties of well-trained and thoroughly disciplined regular troops to operate effectively behind the enemy lines can be out of all proportion to the numbers involved.

(b) That the operations of these uniformed troops are quite distinct from special non-regular parties such as SOE, Secret Service of Political Parties also often introduced behind the enemy lines by dropping from the air.

This type of operation is, therefore, as yet only in its infancy and the possibilities for development are enormous.

There is, therefore, a place in the British Army organisation for SAS Troops: that is, troops trained to fight and carry out military tasks in small isolated parties behind the enemy lines.

SAS Troops are trained to operate either by land, sea or air. That they should be airborne is necessary because often they will not otherwise be able to reach their objective.

PRINCIPLES

16. Before considering the possible role of SAS Troops it is necessary to specify certain principles and factors which must influence their employment.

The employment of SAS Troops, especially in the planning stage, will be strategic more often than tactical. SAS activities should, therefore, be an integral part (however small) of the main plan rather than a diversionary role allotted at a later stage. In this connection a clear charter exists for SAS Troops where there are important tasks which cannot conveniently or economically be tackled by regular formations and, more particularly, which lie far behind the enemy lines or present particular difficulties of access.

17. Principles

(a) Intervention by SAS Troops must have a strategic or tactical effect on operations. The degree of risk that should be accepted depends on the importance of the task.

(b) It is invidious to state that such a task is or is not an SAS role, but it is essential to consider whether the task allotted cannot be carried out with greater chance of success by other military units or other branches of the Services (Air Force etc).

This applies particularly to diversionary tasks or attacks on specific pin-pointed tasks in a tactical area.

(c) The very high degree of individual and collective training makes it possible to operate in smaller parties than troops not specially trained for this role with equal or greater effect.

(d) Where troops are operating behind the enemy lines, they should be scattered in as many small parties as possible, though having where possible good communication by signal or courier with a small central base.

(e) Good signal communications are essential and only under very exceptional circumstances is it sound to land parties without some form of signal communication.

(f) Parties must have a firm plan for their eventual withdrawal, however vital the target.

(g) SAS Troops can rarely achieve their objective if landed in the face of immediate and alert ground opposition.
(h) The initiative must be retained as long as possible by operating in an offensive manner. The psychological importance of keeping the morale high, both of own troops and of local partisans and civilians who may be assisting them, is enormous.
(j) Surprise should be achieved and exploited fully. For this reason operations are normally carried out at night.
(k) Casualties can and should be kept at a low percentage, bearing in mind that all personnel captured may be shot.

ROLE

19. SAS Troops, after initial landing by sea, air or land infiltration, are trained to operate in such numbers as are most suitable for the task in hand. They can be employed in either a strategic or tactical role, and their work bears a close similarity to that of Mosquito aircraft in the Royal Air Force.
20. Strategic
Strategic employment gives more scope for small parties to fulfil the first essential of any detachment. That is to contain a larger force of the enemy than the detachment concerned. For SAS Troops to pay a proper dividend their role must be tied up with the main strategical plan.

Primary tasks are:
(a) Communications. Continuous harassing of enemy lines of communications to delay movement of enemy reserves and supplies by demolition of railways, roads and signals.
(b) Attacking and Harassing. Attacks on enemy headquarters, patrols, fuel installations and dumps. General reduction of enemy morale.
(c) Attacks on dispersed aircraft on airfields.
(d) Intelligence. Reports on enemy movements and dispositions. Survey work on enemy defences, minefields, state of bridges, etc.
(e) Bombing Targets. To supply targets for allied air forces, and if FCPs or VGPs can be used to direct aircraft on to targets.
(f) Resistance. To assist in the organisation and training of Resistance, so that larger parties can be landed at a later date when more overt action by Resistance is required.
(g) Diversionary. To tie up or draw off enemy forces from the main battle area.

In strategic areas it is easier to select suitable terrain where enemy troops are not so thick on the ground; that time factor is not likely to be so vital; the selection of suitable DZs or landing points by sea is simplified; resupply by air is also easier unless enemy fighter aircraft opposition is very active. The difficulties of co-ordinating plans with own front line troops does not arise.

Final withdrawal may, however, prove more difficult if the parties cannot be over-run by own troops within a specified time.

21. Tactical

It is obviously more difficult for small parties to achieve surprise and operate successfully in the immediate battle area, where enemy troops are thick on the ground, and their period of operating must, therefore, be short and depend on accurate timing and employment at the opportune moment. The selection of suitable DZs for airborne operations will be more difficult owing to enemy and own anti-aircraft fire.

The necessity of terrain being suitable becomes an even more important factor. It is unlikely that parties will have many worth while targets during a static period, but far greater opportunities occur when the position is fluid.

Possible tasks are:

(a) Harassing and Ambushing. During an offensive and at the opportune moment parties can be dropped or infiltrated by land and operate for a short period against enemy lines of communications, railways, roads, signals and headquarters and help considerably to delay the enemy withdrawal and add to his confusion.

(b) Intelligence. Parties landed by air or infiltrated by land can operate for 2/3 days behind the enemy lines and send back information on enemy gun positions, etc.

(c) Bombing Targets. (See 20(e)). To supply targets etc.

(d) Large Scale Airborne Operations. Parties can be dropped on an outer circle to work back to airborne bridgehead, or can be landed with jeeps in the airborne bridgehead on a reconnaissance role. If security restrictions permitted, SAS parties landed in advance could provide reception or guides for a major airborne or seaborne landing.

(e) Reconnaissance. Jeep parties can either work on the flank of main advance in a role very similar to that of a reconnaissance regiment or, if conditions are suitable, infiltrate behind the enemy lines. A jeep force may be of special value after a sea landing or river crossing where enemy defences are weak and quick penetration is possible, before the heavier

armoured vehicles of a reconnaissance regiment can be landed.
(f) Anti-demolitions. To prevent enemy demolitions of bridges, dumps, etc. It is unlikely if enemy opposition is strong that a small SAS party could successfully attack and hold any pin-pointed target such as RDF station, battery position, bridge, etc. At the same time the threat of possible landings of SAS parties will tie up a considerable number of enemy troops, and any landing of small SAS parties in a tactical area is likely for a short period to be mistaken for a major airborne landing and to have an exaggerated effect.
22. The employment of SAS Troops in their present set-up during a large-scale withdrawal has not yet been tested. Their role would be very similar to that allotted to HQ Auxiliary Units in ENGLAND when a German invasion was contemplated. They could undoubtedly achieve similar results in delaying enemy spear-points by harassing his comparatively unprotected lines of communication, carrying out demolitions and in supplying information.

The problem of withdrawal would be difficult, though developments in "Pick-Up" operations by the Air Force might simplify this considerably.

PART V – ADMINISTRATION

GENERAL

81. SAS operations demand a very highly organised system of resupply to meet the requirements of parties in the Field at short notice, often less than 24 hours.

CLOTHING, EQUIPMENT, WEAPONS, AMMUNITION AND SUPPLIES.

85. A list of specialised articles of arms, equipment, etc. above normal scales that are required to be held by SAS Troops are listed below. The actual amount of arms, equipment, etc. carried by any party will vary considerably according to the nature of the operation.

(a) Arms

This list shows the variety of arms used on operations in NORTH WEST EUROPE. The weight factor and resupply of ammunition are important factors. Heavier weapons as listed in paragraph (iii) are invaluable on certain types of operations.

(i) Personal Weapons.

Pistols–Colt .45.
Browning 9 mm.
Carbines–US .30 (folding butt).
or Sten Mk V
or TSMG

(ii) Additional Weapons according to nature of Operation.

Rifle No.4 Mk I.
Rifle No.4 Mk I (T) (Snipers).
Guns Machine–Bren .303 Mk III (one per 3/4 all ranks).
Lightened Bren (if possible).
Bren (lightweight).
IMG–Browning M2 HB Flexed .50.
Vickers .303 GO No.1 Mk I Cable operated Special Mountings available for use on jeeps.
or Browning .303 Mk II.
PIAT Mk I
or Launchers Rocket (Bazooka).
Pistols Signal No. 1 Mk III.
Mk V.
Ordnance ML–2" Mortar.
3" Mortar.
Ordnance SB–4.2" Mortar.
.75 Pack Howitzer.

(iii) Special Weapons.

Wellrod.
Pistols. .25.
.45 De Lisle Silent Carbine.
.30 Silent Carbine.
Patchett.

(iv) Grenades.

No. 36 Mk I T
75 Mk I A/Tk
77 Mk I Smoke (WP)
77 Mk II Smoke (CASM)
79 Mk I Smoke (WF)
82 Mk I PZD 247 (Gammon)
Hand made Lewis bomb – 1lb Plastic mixed with Thermite and a time pencil.

(v) Mines.

Mines contact A/T HE Mk V HC- C/W Fuses
(Mines contact A/T HE Mk V HC- W/C Fuzes
(Fuze mine contact No. 3 Mk I

(vi) Explosives.

See list at Paragraph 86.

(b) Clothing and Equipment.

(i) Clothing

Smocks Deniston
Coats Duffle
Puttees
Boots Ammunition – PHILLIPS rubber soles, insoles felt.
Coats Jeep Driver Waterproof

(ii) Equipment (personal)

Bags Sleeping Airborne
  Bedding Rolls Cover
Bags Sleeping Icelandic
  Covers waterproof No.1 for 3lb Sleeping Bag.
Body Armour Sets
Haversack USA Pattern
Rucksack Bergen
  Pads Shoulder Rucksack
or Carriers Everest Mk II Folding Platform
Kitbags Special Airborne
  Ropes Kitbag
  Sleeves Rope
  Jettison Quick Release
  Belts Quick Release
Ropes C/W Toggle 6' 6"
Tents Arctic 2-men
  8-men

(iii) Equipment (Technical).

Compasses Prismatic Liquid Mk III (one per man)
Binoculars Prismatic No.2)
or No.5) one per 2/3 men
or 2½ x 50–10 Field)
Watches Wristlet
or GS TP – one per man

Knives Fighting Airborne
'A' Force Special Lock Knives
Escape Aid Kit
Cutters Wire Folding
or Cutters Wire 8"
Irons Tree Climbing
Cases Map P Type
Protractors Ivorine (one per 5/10 all ranks)
Torches Usalite TL 122A
Air Sea Rescue Lamps
Holophane Lights
Aldis Lamps
Cookers Portable No.2
or No.3
Flasks Thermos No.81
Trolleys Folding Airborne
Bicycles Folding Airborne
Rubber Dinghies (RAF Pattern)

(iv) Medical.
Special Medical Pack.

(v) RASC.
Special 24 hour Ration Packs
Stock Commodities – See paragraph 87 (Sheet 33).

(vi) Airborne.
Parachutes X Type 28"
32" (small number)
Containers CLE Mk III
H
C
Panniers
or Bundles
Jeep Crates and Crashpans
Jeep Clusters

86. Explosives.

Serial No.	Item.		Serial No.	Item.	
531	P.H.E.		532	Thermite	
533	Primers CE/TNT 1	cm	534	Cordtex Plastic	feet
535	Dets, No.27 or 8		536	Dets, No.33, Electric	

537 Safety Fuze feet
538 Instantaneous Fuze, Orange feet
539 Igniter S.F., Percussion
540 Tubes, Fuze, Sealing
541 Trip Wire, .014 x 50 yds reels
542 Trip Wire, .032 x 25 yds reels
543 Switches, Push
544 Switches, Pull
545 Switches, Release
546 Switches, No.8, Anti-Personnel
547 Matches, Fuzes
548 Cap Sealing Compound tins
549 Crimpers
550 Spades, Parachutists
551 Magazines, Detonator, (Pull)
552 Igniters Copper Tubes
553 Magnets
554 Vaseline tubes
555 Incendiary P.T. Black
556 Incendiary P.T. Red
557 Incendiary P.T. White
558 Incendiary P.T. Green
559 Switch, Time, No 10, Black
560 " " " Red
561 " " " White
562 " " " Green
563 " " " Yellow
564 " " " Blue
565 Igniter Fuze Fog Signal
566 Tyre Bursters
567 Fabric Rubberized yds
568 Solution, Rubber tubes
569 Tape Adhesive rolls
570 Cable, Electric, Durotwinflex feet
571 Balloons Long
572 Boards Striker
573 "General Wades"
574 Limpets
575 G.C. Primers
576 Fire Pots, 1¾ lb
577 Switches, Pressure
578 Ammanol lbs
579 Tyre Bursters, Mk II
580 Prima Cord feet

87. R.A.S.C. Commodities.

ANTI-FREEZE (GALLONS)
AFV BISCUITS (10 oz TINS)
AFV PACKS (2 MEN)
ARCTIC RATIONS (48 hrs)
BISCUITS SERVICE (lbs)
CANDLES (STICK)
CIGARETTES (DUTY FREE)
CIGARETTES (FRENCH ISSUE)
CIGARETTES (TINS OF 20)
CIGARETTES (ISSUE)
COMPO RATIONS (14 MEN)
SALT (lbs)
SUGAR (lbs)
SHAVING SOAP (STICKS)
SOUPS (S.H. TINS)
SWEETS BOILED F (lbs)
SWEETS BOILED ISSUE (lbs)
TOBACCO (lbs)
TEA (lbs)
TOOTH PASTE (TINS)
HEXAMINE COOKERS
24 hr RATIONS

CHOCOLATE (lbs)
COFFEE (lbs)
COCOA (S.H. TINS)
CORNED BEEF (12 oz TINS)
CHEESE (30 oz)
CHEWING GUM (PKTS)
DRIPPING SPREAD (2 oz TINS)
EMERGENCY RATIONS
FLOUR (lbs)
MATCHES (BOXES)
MATCHES (BOOKLETS)
MARGARINE (lbs)
MEAT EXTRACT (lbs)
NAAFI PACKS SPECIAL
OATMEAL (lbs)
PEMMICAN (lbs)
HEXAMINE REFILLS
RUM (GALLONS)

WATER S OUTFITS
WHISKEY (BOTTLES)
TOILET ROLLS
COMPOUND VITAMIN TABLETS
FLOUR (CULINARY lbs)
RAISONS [sic] (2 oz PKTS)
COOKING FAT (lbs)
MILK (16 oz TINS)
PEPPER (lbs)
MUSTARD (lbs)
LUNCHEON MEAT (12 oz TINS)
SARDINES (4 oz TINS)
EGGS DRIED (lbs)
CARROTS DEH. (lbs)
CABBAGE DEH. (lbs)
BAKING POWDER (lbs)
CUSTARD POWDER (lbs)

<u>PERSONNEL</u>

88. There has been no great difficulty, whenever the necessary facilities for visiting Regiments, Holding Units, IBDs etc in Great Britain or abroad have been granted of enrolling volunteers for SAS Regiments. There is no doubt that for the type of work which they will be called upon to perform, they must be highly disciplined and exceptionally well trained and led. Generally speaking a party of three or four specialists is as good as a party of twelve or fifteen normal good soldiers led by one officer. The size of the party is little guide to its operational efficiency. Experience is naturally a great asset and the most successful operation personnel have been from 23 – 35 years old. The most successful parties have been led by men, who have great individualism, and who have experience of foreign countries. Languages help a great deal, and it is for this reason probably that the University man, who has travelled and led an independent career has often proved to be the best leader.

Initiative, individuality, and a strong sense of discipline and responsibility are the main characteristics required. It is argued that a unit like an SAS Regiment takes its pick of the Army and is therefore an expensive force. This is not necessarily the case, as the individual training given often enables Commanders to train up young officers and men to a higher degree of maturity than is possible in a normal unit. Similarly these men with great individuality do not always fit in to best advantage in an Infantry Battalion, where they may not at times get full scope for their activities.

It is worthy of note that a high percentage of men in both 1 and 2 SAS Regiments are Regulars.

89. Guides.
It is unlikely if operating in a foreign country that many of the SAS Troops will speak the language: It is important therefore to attach and train with the unit nationals of the country concerned, who can accompany parties on operations.

One of the features of the SAS Troops in NW Europe has been its international nature with French and Belgians under command while small detachments of Dutch and Norwegians were attached for operational purposes.

There is great scope for the future in attaching detachments from all parts of the Empire, and by this means a useful link would be established in time of peace which would increase the operational value of SAS Troops in time of war especially when required at short notice to operate in theatres outside Europe.

90. Percentage of casualties.
SAS operations in NW Europe have shown that on an average casualties including wounded, who can be treated on the spot, and continue to operate, should not exceed 15–20 per cent, but a considerably higher percentage might be expected, if parties were operating in unfriendly enemy territory.

These figures show that SAS Troops are not an expensive force to maintain, though there may be lengthier periods especially when climatic conditions are unfavourable, when SAS Troops as compared to normal infantry Troops cannot operate advantageously.

For reasons of morale and in view of the time required to train what are specialist troops, a higher rate of casualties except on a few priority operations, would be unsound.

91. Summary.
It is unsound to compare their role with that of infantry. They are specialists and when operating have a more intricate and specialised

job, but have compensating advantages. It is, however, essential to keep the "offensive spirit" which is the keynote to success on operations at the highest level. To achieve this it is of the utmost importance that the facilities for inculcating the best 'esprit' and for giving the best training are made available even if the unit may appear at times to get preferential treatment.

PART VI. – TACTICS AND TRAINING

JEEPS.

97. In order to give this mobility, specially modified jeeps were dropped by parachute (70/80) or landed by Glider (in BRITTANY) or infiltrated through the enemy lines or on his flank. These Jeeps were landed with extra petrol-tanks to give a range of 600/700 miles and had special armour plating to protect personnel. Equipped with Twin-Vickers .303 mounting in front, Browning .30 or Vickers .303 at rear, and on occasions with Bren LMG and Mortars 3" (carried by every third jeep), they had very strong firing power and were invaluable. Jeeps are necessarily expendable and a casualty rate to jeeps of up to 40 percent must be anticipated on operations extending over 3 to 4 weeks, but in most cases even if the jeeps were knocked out, personnel were able to get away safely. The presence of jeeps in an area soon becomes known to the enemy and security is prejudiced, but it has been found possible to hide the jeeps successfully and with the extra mobility given to the party, the base can be moved more often, a compensating advantage. The jeeps were also useful on DZ's in moving supplies etc., to hide-out.

FURTHER READING

Allan, Stuart. *Commando Country*. NMS Enterprises Limited: Edinburgh, 2007.
Cowles, Virginia. *The Phantom Major: The Story of David Stirling and the S.A.S. Regiment*. Collins: London, 1958.
Dillon, Martin and Bradford, Roy. *Rogue Warrior of the SAS: The Blair Mayne Legend*. John Murray: London, 1987.
Farran, Roy. *Winged Dagger: Adventures on Special Service*. Collins: London, 1948.
Geraghty, Tony. *Who Dares Wins: The Special Air Service, 1950 to the Falklands*. Arms and Armour Press: London, 1983.
Gordon, John W. *The Other Desert War: British Special Forces in North Africa, 1940–1943*. Greenwood Press: Connecticut, 1987.
Harrison, D.I. *These Men are Dangerous: The S.A.S. at War*. Cassell: London, 1957.
Hoe, Alan. *David Stirling: The Authorised Biography of the Creator of the SAS*. Little, Brown and Company: London, 1992.
Kemp, Anthony. *The SAS at War 1941–1945*. John Murray: London, 1991.
Kemp, Peter. *No Colours or Crest*. Cassell: London, 1958.
Ladd, James D. *SAS Operations: More than Daring*. (2nd edition.) Robert Hale: London, 1999.
Lewes, John. *Jock Lewes: Co-founder of the SAS*. Leo Cooper: Barnsley, 2001.
McMichael, Major Scott R. *A Historical Perspective on Light Infantry*. Research Survey No. 6. Combat Studies Institute, U.S. Army Command and General Staff College: Fort Leavenworth, 1987.
Morris, Eric. *Guerrillas in Uniform: Churchill's Private Armies in the Middle East and the War Against Japan, 1940–45*. Hutchinson: London, 1989.
Mortimer, Gavin. *Stirling's Men: The Inside History of the SAS in World War II*. Weidenfeld & Nicolson, London, 2004.
Ross, Hamish. *Paddy Mayne: Lt Col Blair 'Paddy' Maine, 1 SAS Regiment*. Sutton: Stroud, 2003.
Seymour, William. *British Special Forces: The Story of Britain's Undercover Soldiers*. Sidgwick and Jackson: London, 1985.
Stevens, Gordon. *The Originals: The Secret History of the Birth of the SAS in their Own Words*. Ebury Press: London, 2006.
Strawson, John. *A History of the S.A.S. Regiment*. Secker & Warburg: London, 1984.
Warner, Philip. *The SAS: The Official History*. Sphere Books: London, 1983.
Wellsted, Ian. *SAS with the Maquis: In Action with the French Resistance*, June–September 1944. Greenhill: London, 1994.

SOURCE NOTES

PRIMARY SOURCES

The Liddell Hart Centre for Military Archives (LHCMA) at King's College London holds the private papers of hundreds of senior defence personnel who served from 1900 onwards, including many who helped to develop or who served with Special Forces units during World War II. The collection consists of a wide range of material, from texts of lectures and memoranda to operational maps and plans.

The UK's National Archives in Kew, London, catalogues the daily record of events, reports on operations and exercises, intelligence summaries, and so on (more than 250 files in total) of the Special Air Service during World War II under reference WO 218, for "War Office: Special Services War Diaries, Second World War". There are further SAS-related documents catalogued separately and these include: AIR 20 and AIR 37 (Air Ministry: Allied Expeditionary Air Force, later Supreme Headquarters Allied Expeditionary Force [Air]); WO 201 (which includes "L" Detachment); WO 204 (which includes operations in Italy); WO 219 (which includes involvement in Operation Overlord); WO 361 (which includes Enquiries into Missing Personnel); and WO 373 (which includes Recommendations for Honours and Awards). The surviving records of the various organisations that ran active operations of sabotage and subversion behind enemy lines, including the Special Operations Executive (SOE), are catalogued under reference HS 8.

CHAPTER 1

All from Lieutenant-Colonel Colin McVean Gubbins's "The Art of Guerilla Warfare", War Office, London, 1939. Gubbins's personal papers are archived at the Imperial War Museum, London.

CHAPTER 2

Offensive Demolitions. Lochailort Fieldcraft Course, Lectures 1 and 6 (December 1940, January 1941, March 1941). These extracts are dated, collectively, to March 1941, from the papers of General Sir Hugh Charles Stockwell, reference 3/2, LHCMA.

CHAPTER 3

Memorandum on the Origins of the Special Air Service by Col. David Stirling, DSO, OBE, 8 November 1948. These selected points 7–21 inclusive, from an original 1–22, are part of a Staff College Camberley 1948 course "History of SAS" from the papers of General Sir Roderick McLeod (1905–1980), "Papers relating

to operations of the Special Air Service (SAS) during World War Two, and to its formation, 1944–1948", reference 1/10, LHCMA.

CHAPTER 4

Papers relating to raids by Lt Col (Archibald) David Stirling, Commanding Officer, Special Air Service, including notes by Robert Edward Laycock on Stirling's raids on enemy aerodromes and extract from a letter from Maj Randolph Churchill, Special Air Service, to Prime Minister Winston (Leonard Spencer) Churchill giving a detailed account of a raid on Benina airfield near Benghazi, Libya, led by Stirling, 24 June 1942. From the papers of Major General Sir Robert Edward Laycock (1907–1968), "Papers relating to Commando operations 1941 Apr–[1944]", reference LAYCOCK 5/14, LHCMA.

CHAPTER 5

"Toughest Job in the War" by Gordon Gaskill ("by cable from Cairo"), July 1942. From *The American Magazine* July 1942, pages 11, 101 and 102.

CHAPTER 6

Papers of Capt George Jellicoe, Special Air Service Regiment, Middle East, reporting on the possibilities for small-scale raids in the Eastern Mediterranean, 1 January 1943. From the papers of Major General Sir Robert Edward Laycock (1907–1968), "Papers on Special Service Brigade following the disbandment of LAYFORCE, [1941-1946]", reference LAYCOCK 4/11, LHCMA.

CHAPTER 7

War Department Technical Manual TM 9-803 "¼-ton 4x4 Truck (Willys-Overland Model MB and Ford Model GPW)" was issued by the US War Department on 22 February 1944, superseding manual TB 9-803-4 of 5 January 1944. United States Government Printing Office, Washington DC.

CHAPTER 8

"The Bren Light Machine Gun: Description, Use and Mechanism" manual (undated) was originally printed and published by Gale & Polden of Aldershot, UK.

CHAPTER 9

"Looking Back to the French S.A.S. in Brittany, 1944" is a typescript memorandum on the exploits of the Special Air Service (SAS) in France. It is from the papers of General Sir Roderick McLeod (cited above), reference 1/8, LHCMA, dated 8 November 1948. Upon the typescript is a handwritten note: "Written by Lt. Col. Oas Cary-Elwes, then major C-E." Lt Col Oswald Aloysius Joseph Cary-Elwes (1913–1994), 20 Liaison Headquarters, SAS Brigade, was parachuted into Brittany, France, in June 1944 to make contact with SAS and Maquis units.

CHAPTER 10

"Operations of the 4th French Parabattalion" is from the papers of General Sir Roderick McLeod (cited above), undated, reference 1/2, LHCMA. The memorandum relates to the operations of 4th SAS in Brittany, France, 5–30 June 1944, for the severance of German communications and the recruitment and arming of resistance groups, including the establishment of bases for operations DINGSON, SAMWEST and GROG.

CHAPTER 11

"Summary of Casualties Inflicted on the Enemy by S.A.S. Troops During Operations in 1944" is from the papers of General Sir Roderick McLeod (cited above), undated, reference 1/1, LHCMA. The memorandum contains statistics compiled from official reports on Axis forces personnel killed, wounded or taken prisoner; transports captured or destroyed; railways, bridges, communications and military installations destroyed; equipment captured; and SAS casualties. The span of dates and areas covered is unclear from the report.

CHAPTER 12

These excerpts are from an original, much longer, five-part (I–V, containing 105 numbered points, many containing alphabetical sub-items a–k, and so on) typescript memorandum entitled "Notes on the organisation, history and employment of Special Air Service troops" [by Lt Col Ian G Collins, General Staff Officer 1 (SAS), 1 Airborne British Corps], containing review of SAS operations in North West Europe, Jun 1944–May 1945; proposals for future organisation of SAS; strategic and tactical roles; planning and preparation of operations, including allotment of aircraft or naval craft, surprise, intelligence, choice of drop zones, casualties and psychological warfare; technical points in the mounting of SAS airborne operations; inter-communications between base and field parties; administration, including clothing, equipment, weapons, ammunition and supplies; tactics and training, including jeeps and heavier weapons. From the papers of General Sir Roderick McLeod (1905–1980), "Papers relating to the SAS following operations in Northern Europe, World War Two, 1945–1958", reference 2/1, LHCMA.

INDEX

Note: page references in *italics* indicate illustrations.

ACKNOWLEDGEMENTS AND PERMISSIONS

Acknowledgements

I am indebted to John Lee at Anova, who originally helped to nurture this book into existence. I owe a further debt of gratitude to Janet Murphy and Jenny Clark at Bloomsbury, who have seen it through to completion. The book would not have been possible without historical archives, so I offer thanks to the following individuals, organizations and institutions for supplying information or pointing me in fruitful directions: Lianne Smith at the Liddell Hart Centre for Military Archives, King's College London; British National Archives, Kew, London; the Department of Printed Books, National Army Museum, Chelsea, London; the Imperial War Museum, London; and the US National Archives and Record Administration, College Park, Maryland, USA. Also, those excellent and highly readable primary and secondary sources listed in the Notes and Further Reading, especially those from the special individuals who pioneered this great unit of the British Army. Although many research leads were received from a variety of sources, I am wholly responsible for any errors of fact or interpretation that remain.